More praise for
the ticking is the bomb

"Flynn recalls and records in a stunningly beautiful cascade of images. . . . A striking collection of memories that will mystify, enlighten, trouble and amaze." —*Kirkus Reviews*, starred review

"Flynn's life is so volcanic and his writing style so kinetic and punchy that others will be drawn into this gripping personal narrative." —*Publishers Weekly*

"[A] finely crafted mosaic of edgy beauty, ambushing drama, and unsparing reflections." —*Booklist*

"Flynn is among those rare souls able to direct the course of his wrath: a poet by training and a Buddhist by disposition, he knows when to gun the engine, letting his passion infuse the prose, and when to pull back, casting an analytical eye on all he sees. In this memoir he has produced an angry book that's about more than just anger. . . . Each book rivets with a pure, unfiltered honesty." —*B&N Review*

"The emotional honesty in Flynn's memoir is as red-blooded as an open wound. It's as if he has shed the protective skin of cynicism or irony, leaving him exposed to both the brutal malignancy of the world as well as its intense beauty. His book is a 'memoir of bewilderment'." —*The Independent*

"Flynn infuses *The Ticking* with a poet's sensibilities, assembling bits and pieces of his life and viewpoints into a pastiche that pulses with humor, humanity, and outrage. His offhand prose brims with roguish winks at his rocky life." —*Texas Monthly*

"Flynn takes the art of the memoir a step forward with his uncompromising new memoir." —*Manchester Journal*

"*The Ticking Is the Bomb* is a penetrating, provocative story of impending fatherhood." —*The Daily Beast*

"As immensely personal as *The Ticking Is the Bomb* is, it pushes readers to acknowledge, if not meditate on, the urges lurking inside us, those we tamp down in order to continue, to resist the impulses (conscious or not) to hurt ourselves, the ones we love, even those we don't. . . . Flynn navigates this murky water through his elegant language. . . . This is not a book of blame, but one of understanding how images and words are manipulated, in personal relationships or in a larger scope." —*The Millions*

books by nick flynn

Another Bullshit Night in Suck City

Some Ether

Blind Huber

A Note Slipped Under the Door
(coauthored with Shirley McPhillips)

Alice Invents a Little Game and Alice Always Wins

the ticking
is the bomb

. . . . *a memoir*

nick flynn

w. w. norton & company

new york   london

Excerpts of this book, often in slightly different form, originally appeared in *Esquire*, *Open City, The Book of Dads* (Ecco Press), and *The Best American Nonrequired Reading 2009* (Mariner Books).

disclaimer: This is a work of nonfiction, but it is also full of dreams, speculations, memories, and shadows. Many names have been changed.

For information about permission to reproduce selections from this book, write to Permissions, W. W. Norton & Company, Inc., 500 Fifth Avenue, New York, NY 10110

For information about special discounts for bulk purchases, please contact W. W. Norton Special Sales at specialsales@wwnorton.com or 800-233-4830

Manufacturing by Courier Westford
Book design by Lovedog Studio
Production manager: Anna Oler

Library of Congress Cataloging-in-Publication Data

Flynn, Nick, 1960–
The ticking is the bomb .... a memoir /
Nick Flynn.— 1st ed.
p. cm.
Includes bibliographical references.
ISBN 978-0-393-06816-0
1. Flynn, Nick, 1960– 2. Poets, American—Biography.
3. Fatherhood. I. Title.
PS3556.L894Z468 2010
811'.6—dc22
[B]

2009034764

ISBN 978-0-393-33886-7 pbk.

W. W. Norton & Company, Inc.
500 Fifth Avenue, New York, N.Y. 10110
www.wwnorton.com

W. W. Norton & Company Ltd.
Castle House, 75/76 Wells Street, London W1T 3QT

1 2 3 4 5 6 7 8 9 0

for maeve, queen of the fairies

the ticking is the bomb

Grain upon grain, one by one, and one day, suddenly,
there's a heap, a little heap, the impossible heap.

—Beckett, *Endgame*

a telegram made of shadows

(2007) This black and white photograph in my hand is an image of my unborn daughter—this, at least, is what I'm told. It's actually a series of photographs, folded one upon the other, like a tiny accordion. I was there when the doctor or technician or whoever he was made it with his little wand of sound. I sat beside him, looked into the screen as he pointed into the shadows—*Can you see her nose, can you see her hand? Can you see her foot, right here, next to her ear?* I was there when each shot was taken, yet in some ways, still, it is all deeply unreal. It's as if I were holding a photograph of a dream, a dream sleeping inside the body of the woman I love—I'll call her Inez—the woman who now walks through the world with two hearts beating inside her.

At this same moment, or outside of this moment, outside of us, out there, in the world, exists another set of photographs. One depicts a naked man being dragged by a soldier out of a cell on the end of a leash. Another depicts a pyramid of hooded, cowering men, also naked. A soldier stands behind this pyramid, his arms folded, smiling. In yet another photograph a blue-eyed girl—also smiling—gives a thumbs-up over a corpse. Hundreds of such photographs exist, by now we've all seen them, by now we've all held them in our hands, but they also have the texture of dreams—shadowy, diaphanous, changeable.

Grain upon grain.

One day I hope to be able to tell my daughter a story about a dark time, the dark days before she was born, and how her coming was a ray of light. *We got lost for a while*, this story will begin, *but then we found our way.*

This, at least, is the version I hope to be able to tell her.

one

a field guide to getting lost

Here's a secret: Everyone, if they live long enough, will lose their way at some point. You will lose your way, you will wake up one morning and find yourself lost. This is a hard, simple truth. If it hasn't happened to you yet consider yourself lucky. When it does, when one day you look around and nothing is recognizable, when you find yourself alone in a dark wood having lost the way, you may find it easier to blame someone else—an errant lover, a missing father, a bad childhood. Or it may be easier to blame the map you were given—folded too many times, out of date, tiny print. You can shake your fist at the sky, call it *fate, karma, bad luck*, and sometimes it is. But, for the most part, if you are honest, you will only be able to blame yourself. Life can, of course, blindside you, yet often as not we choose to be blind—*agency*, some call it. If you're lucky you'll remember a story you heard as a child, the trick of leaving a trail of breadcrumbs, the idea being that after whatever it is that is going to happen in those woods has happened, you can then retrace your steps, find your way back out. But no one said you wouldn't be changed, by the hours, the years, spent wandering those woods.

~

(2005) A year after the Abu Ghraib photographs appear I wake up in Texas one morning, in love with two women, honest with neither. I am finishing up my second semester of teaching poetry at the University of Houston, getting ready to fly back to New York, where both these women are waiting for me, or so I imagine. I'd been "dating" for a few years, since the breakup of a long-term relationship, and more than once it had been made abundantly clear that I was not very good at it. For me, "dating" often felt like reading Tolstoy—exhilarating, but a struggle, at times, to keep the characters straight. The fact that the chaos had been distilled down to two women—one I'll call Anna, the other was Inez—felt, to me, like progress. For months I'd been speaking to one or the other on my cellphone. Her name (or hers) came up on the tiny screen, and each time my heart leapt. It was the end of April. I'd come to the conclusion (delusion?) that if I could just get us all in the same room we could figure out a way it could work out. Another part of me, though, would have been perfectly happy to let it all keep playing out in the shadows.

The book *A Field Guide to Getting Lost* came out around this time—it is, in part, a meditation on the importance, for any creative act, to allow the mind and body to wander. The title jumped out at me—maybe I could use it as sort of an *anti*map. *Lost really has two disparate meanings. Losing things is about the famil-iar falling away, getting lost is about the unfamiliar appearing.* . . . Another book that came out around this time was *Why We Get Lost and How We Find Our Way*, but I didn't pick that one up—perhaps I wasn't ready not to be lost. Lost, at that moment in my life, manifest itself as feeling bewildered, confused, bereft—it's not that I didn't know where I was, I just didn't know what I was doing there. On a deeper level, I knew that my *bereftitude* was only partly due to my self-inflicted disasters of love. Beneath that surface tension was the inescapable fact that I'd just crossed the threshold of being the same age my parents had been when they'd imploded, each in his or her own way. My mother had killed herself when she was forty-two, shot herself in the heart. When my father was forty-five, he fell—drunk—from a ladder while painting a house, an accident which may or may not have left him with a permanent head injury. A year later he'd enter a bank and pass his first forged check, the start of a small-time run that would eventually lead him into federal prison. After doing his time, after being released, he'd drift even deeper into his life of wandering, until he ended up living on the streets for a few years, which is where I got to know him.

And now, here I am, waking up in Texas, just past the age my mother never made it beyond, the same age my father was when he went off the rails. The dream I'm having is already dissolving, and I'm left, once again, with my unquiet mind, which for some months now has been straddling these two beautiful women. It has nothing to do with fate, karma, or bad luck.

handshake

(2005) A few days after I land back in New York I go to a ceremony at Lincoln Center. I'd won an award from PEN, the literary and human rights organization, for a book I'd written that circled around homelessness and my father. I sat in the audience and listened as a citation was read for a writer whose work I was unfamiliar with—he'd won the sister award to mine:

> . . . Sam Harris analyzes the world with a humanist's sympathy, but he has no time for those who murder and torture in the name of beliefs based on ancient concepts that are both unbelievable and, more important, unprovable. . . .

Abu Ghraib was still very much in the news at this point, and, like many others, I was still both confused and enraged by it all. At some point that night, Harris and I exchanged a few words. We're photographed together, shaking hands, smiling. A few months later I read his book, *The End of Faith*, and find that it is, in part, a treatise advocating the use of torture:

> Given what many of us believe about the exigencies of our war on terrorism, the practice of torture, in certain circumstances, would seem to be not only permissible but necessary.

As I read those words, and others like them (*dust off the strappado*, or *it's become ethical to kill people for what they believe*), a switch flips on in my brain. Harris, like anyone, is free to write and publish whatever he wishes, but why did a human rights organization choose to endorse it with an award? And why had they photographed me shaking hands with him, smiling like an idiot?

all I have is a photograph

Here is a photograph of my mother, walking away from a white house, carrying an open can of Schlitz, wearing a blond wig and oversized sunglasses, like Anjelica Huston in *The Grifters*. The man next to her is also carrying an open can of Schlitz— we can only see a sliver of him, but it is enough to recognize him as her brother, my uncle. A toddler is hiding behind this uncle, half his face visible, which is more than enough to recognize him as my brother. My mother's wig, a sliver of an uncle, half a brother—so this is my family. But then, who else would these people be? After all, I found this photograph in a box of my mother's things. The sweater my brother wears, a white v-neck with red and blue trim around the collar and sleeves, is the same sweater I had as a child, given to us by our grandfather, who was rich, who had money, who paid for our tennis lessons, though at home we had blocks of government cheese and a silver gallon can with the words PEANUT BUTTER stenciled on the side. We ate the cheese, but we never opened the can, saving it for the darker days to come.

In the photograph they are walking toward the ocean across my grandfather's yard on First Cliff, in Scituate, Massachusetts, my hometown. My mother calls his house "the big house" (as a child I didn't know that "big house" is another way of saying "prison"). A tiny foot, nearly unnoticed, dangles from someone else's arms, someone outside the picture—this could be my foot, I could be in the other uncle's arms, or I could be in the arms of my mother's boyfriend at the time, though I don't know which boyfriend it would be. My foot is so small it is even possible I'm in my father's arms, but he is the last one I imagine.

~

Last night I had a dream: I'm on the phone, but the phone is broken—it is simply an earpiece, a black disc, wires sprouting from it, breaking up in my hands. I have to move it between my ear and my mouth to listen and talk. I am talking to my mother, we are making a plan for me to come to dinner. *What can I bring*, I ask her—*salad? dessert?*

Bring food, she says, *we need food.*

crank

(2005) A photograph of me shaking hands with Sam Harris now exists. Now it will never not exist. After I read his book and discover that he is an advocate of the use of torture (specifically against Muslims), I become, seemingly overnight, a crank. I begin what will become several months of letter writing—to the *New York Times*, to PEN, to Harris, even to the judges who awarded him the prize, who wrote in their citation that . . . *he has no time for those who murder and torture in the name of beliefs based on ancient concepts* . . . I ask the judges if, among other things, they feel that Harris is, perhaps, more forward-looking in his protorture stance. The judges do not respond to my questions.

I read the reviews of *The End of Faith*:

One reviewer feels that the book has ". . . a pointed sense of humor."

Another writes that ". . . despite its polemic edge, this is a happy book."

My personal favorite describes it as ". . . a trip down Memory Lane."

A book that advocates torture is *a trip down Memory Lane*—perhaps an unintentionally accurate description of the secret history of America.

———————

At some point, in the following months, after the award and the photograph and the book reviews and the judges' citation, I tell my friend Claudia that I'm feeling a little nuts, as if I'm seeing something that everyone else insists isn't there.

That's how black people feel all the time, Claudia says with a shrug.

my repertoire

My mother told me a story, just once, of how as a girl she'd been
tied to a chair, the chair teetering at the top of the attic stairs,
her captors, her brothers, threatening to send her end over end,
tumbling down. I don't know if they did this more than once,
and I don't know what they wanted—a question answered, a
promise made—beyond the usual childhood cruelties, or if they
ever got it. Her family had money, so much money that an oil
painting of her—in pigtails, standing beside a horse—hung over
a mantel. She spent her afternoons in stables, was sent away to
private schools, was called a *debutante*. Her father had grown
up with money, her mother had grown up poor—both, alas,
to varying degrees, were drunks. From my mother I got the
sense that her childhood was one of sporadic chaos followed by
long stretches of simple neglect. No one, in spite of—or maybe
because of—all that money, was steering the boat.

At seventeen she met my father, got pregnant, jumped ship.

My father—ah yes, my father. A whole book could be written about my father (or so he thinks), and his stories. The two
are nearly inseparable by now, the same handful, over and
over—his repertoire. A liar always tells his story the same way,
except some—most—of my father's stories have, improbably,
turned out to be true. The story of robbing a few banks. The

story of the novel he's spent his whole life writing. The story of his father inventing the life raft—all true. I first heard these stories, or pieces of them, during those five years he lived on the streets. I was working in the shelter where he'd sometimes spend his nights, and we'd sometimes talk, but he was—is— a grandiose drunk, and so I was not inclined to believe much of what he said. In one of his stories he claimed to be a direct descendant of the Romanovs, of the missing czarina—a delusion, in terms of popularity, just behind claiming to be Jesus. Or Satan.

One of my father's stories, one I found too bizarre to engage with at all, was of being locked up in federal prison for two years, which is true, but while there he claims to have been tortured—experimented on, sleep-deprived, drugged, sexually humiliated—and I don't know if this is true or not. Understand, it is hard and getting harder to get a straight answer from my father, as his alcoholism slips into its twilight stage. When I ask him about his prison time now, he looks wildly around the room or park or coffee shop and whispers, *I can't talk about that here.*

my teufelsberg

(*2007*) This morning, in my inbox, I find this note from a friend in Berlin:

> I was standing on the Teufelsberg (the Devil's Mountain) with a friend last night, listening to Patti Smith playing in the stadium below, and I thought of you. The Teufelsberg is made from all the junk of the war, the broken houses and so on. It is a big mountain, and we stood there looking out over my strange and terrible and beautiful city. Where are you?

Teufelsberg. Devil's Mountain. All the junk of the war.

Here I am, I think, writing about my mother again (*samsara*). And here I am, writing about my father again, building my own Devil's Mountain, piling up all the junk of the war. If asked I'll sometimes say that I'm writing about torture, but I've found that if I say the word "torture" many go glassy-eyed, silent, as if I'd just dropped a stone into a deep, deep well. Sometimes I say I'm writing about my unborn daughter, about my impending fatherhood—five months to go, the clock's ticking—but I don't want to jinx it. I want this book to be behind me before she arrives. I don't want my first days with her to be wrapped up in torture, in shadows. I'm lucky, though—when I turn away from the book, Inez is there, radiantly pregnant, seemingly more sure of what's to come, and this calms me. The baby is, after all, inside her, inside her body—perhaps this makes it more real, for her. But then, Inez has always been this way—certain, or at least seemingly so. It confused me when we first got together, for it seemed that whether I was to stay or go she would be alright, that she would survive. When we were first together I had to face the uncomfortable realization that I wasn't used to calling love something that didn't involve disaster.

Some people tell me that once the baby comes I will feel a new love, a love like I have never felt before. Hearing this, I smile and nod, but it always makes me uneasy. What if I don't feel this love, what if it doesn't happen to me? I'm sure it doesn't—can't—happen to everyone, and that the ones who don't feel it simply don't talk about it. What if I turn out to be one of them? What if I feel it one day and then don't the next day? What if it's fleeting?

Sometimes, if asked, I'll say that I'm writing about the way photographs are a type of dream, about how shadows can end up resembling us, and sometimes I'll say I'm writing a memoir of bewilderment, and just leave it at that, but what I mean is the bewilderment of waking up, my hand on Inez's belly, as the fine points of waterboarding are debated on public radio. But maybe talking about torture is easier than talking about my impending fatherhood, the idea of which, some days, sends me into a tailspin.

Maybe I should tell anyone who asks that I'm writing about

Proteus, the mythological creature who changes shape as you hold on to him, who changes into the shape of that which most terrifies you, as you ask him your question, as you refuse to let go. The question is, often, simply a variation of, *How do I get home?*

pleiad

(1999) For two weeks one summer I swam every day in a small lake on top of a mountain in Vermont. The lake's name is Pleiad, which made me think of the Seven Sisters, the star cluster. I'd wake up early each morning, drive up the mountain, park on the side of the road, and hike fifteen minutes up a narrow trail, all so I could be in the water by seven. No one else was ever there, not at that time, the sun just catching the outcroppings of granite at the far corner, wisps of steam rising off the surface. I was at a writers' conference, and it seemed that everyone was drinking except me. I'd had my last drink ten years earlier, a couple years after my father had ended up on the streets (maybe because my father had ended up on the streets). Swimming, I'd tell anyone who asked, was my Prozac.

The reason for my anxiety was, in part, that the long-term relationship I was in, with a woman I'll call Justine, was limping to its painful, perhaps necessary, end. That it was ending badly (I still cannot imagine a way it could have ended well, though I know this isn't true) drove me to my knees—no, it drove me to swimming pools, to ponds, I threw my body in and swam, hour after hour, I swam for as long as it took, until I had a good thought, just one good thought. Some days, most days, it would take a long time, but finally it was as if I could see it coming across the surface of the water toward me, and as I pulled myself toward it, my body would slowly return—I could feel it again, my body, I could feel myself returning to it, and then, as that one good thought reached me, as I let it wash over me, my body would slowly dissolve. I could feel it—everything—if briefly, and it was enough, it had to be enough. If I didn't make it to the water, if I missed a day, then I knew I wouldn't have that one good thought and, I feared, maybe never have another one again. By certain—most—reckoning, I was to blame, though for a long time I actually held on to the desperate belief that I'd been the one most wronged.

To escape the writing conference, some days, I'd go to Pleiad Lake twice, if someone else wanted to go, if we could find another hour in the afternoon. Some of those who went with me wouldn't even go into the water. They were happy to just hike in and see the lake, which is how I found out that some people don't like to swim, or, more accurately, that some people are afraid of water. I began to ask about this fear, which is how I found out that even some of those who swam were afraid. One told me that she preferred to swim in pools, where you could always see where the water ended. One said he preferred to swim in the ocean, where the salt kept him afloat. One was afraid of what was submerged beneath the surface, of the hidden branch that might snag her leg. Many seemed to be afraid of some unnamed creature that would reach up, bite them, pull them under. Leeches were a fear, though I met no one who had ever been bitten by one. One seemed to be afraid of himself, afraid he would just give up and sink in the middle of the lake. One was afraid of running out of energy and getting pulled over the tiny waterfall. One was afraid of his heart failing and not being able to make it back to shore. From talking about it I realized that I was also afraid, only not of what *was* there, but of what *wasn't* there—my fear was more a type of *horror vacui*, the fear of empty space, the fear of the nothing that is. With my goggles on I could see into the darkness rising up from the unseen bottom, and it was as if I were looking into the universe, the way it just seemed to go on and on. Looking into this empty space, all I could hear was my own breathing, as if that was all there was, and it just didn't seem enough.

the banishment prize

(2001) A year after the relationship with Justine ends, I get a poetry grant, which has one stipulation: in order to get the money I have to leave North America for one year—*the Banishment Prize*, I call it. I end up based for the next two years in Rome. I find a big cheap apartment near Piazza Vittorio, where I plan to finish up the book on homelessness and my father. I buy a beat-up Vespa, and begin dating an Italian playwright. It's hard to complain, except that I'd left a support system I'd spent the last ten years building up, a web of friends and routines that seemed to have kept me, mostly, on an even keel. Without knowing it, and without seeking it, once I landed in Rome this support system began to slowly unravel, to break apart, like those photographs of Antarctica's icecaps falling into the sea. It should also be said that this personal crisis was nearly invisible to those around me, especially since the one who had been closest to me for the past eight years—Justine—was no longer there. But this might be another delusion, the delusion that no one else could see how fucked-up I was, when it is just as likely I came across as an utter mess.

Before I left for Rome, as summer ended, I had a month to swim in a pond in Truro. In the spring, when the pond was swollen with rain, there was no beach, but now, at the end of summer, with the water low, there was a small strip of sand two or three people could crowd onto. For a week or so, every day, I sat next to a woman on this tiny strip of sand, and sometimes we'd talk, and it turned out we knew people in common. On the last day, she invited me to her house for tea, then or whenever I felt like it. *I'd like that*, I said—*I'll come by after my banishment ends.* And I would have, I wanted to but, incomprehensibly, she'd been in the first plane to hit the World Trade Center.

both towers

When both towers were still standing I stopped in a parking lot on Great Jones Street with the rest, watching smoke pour from the one we could see. *What happened*, I asked a stranger, as masses of people streamed past us, all heading north up Lafayette, but he didn't know. At that point no one knew—we were all mere onlookers at that point, smoke filling the sky. Whatever had happened was still happening. In my mind the people streaming northward were all coming from the burning tower, and I was relieved that everyone had made it out alright—that's how my mind translated that beautiful blue day punctured by smoke.

A few minutes later the guy I get my coffee from told me that airplanes had crashed into both towers. *Both towers?* A few minutes after that I stood with another crowd of strangers inside an appliance store on Broadway and watched the first tower fall on a bank of televisions. I could have stood on the sidewalk outside the store and seen it fall, but I thought there might be some words coming from the televisions that would make it all make sense.

proteus

Proteus lives at the bottom of a steep cliff, down a treacherous path, at the edge of the sea. From the top of the cliff you can see him, lolling on a flat rock, staring into the endless nothing of the sea, but to reach him is difficult. You've been told that he has the answer to your question, and you are a little desperate to have this question answered. As you make your way down you must be careful not to dislodge any loose gravel, careful not to cry out when the thorns pierce your feet. You must approach him as quietly as you can, get right up on him, get your hands on him, around his neck. You've been told that you have to hold on while you ask your question, you've been told that you can't let go. You've been told that as you hold on Proteus will transform into the shape and form of that which most terrifies you, in order to get you to release your grip. But the promise is that if you can hold on, through your fear, he will return to his real form and answer your question.

welcome to the year
of the monkey

(2004) I hear word of the photographs before I see the photographs, I hear about them on the car radio. The man on the radio says the words *abu ghraib*, words I've never heard before—at this point I don't know if *abu ghraib* is one word or two, a building or a city, a place or an idea. The man on the radio has seen the photographs, he talks as if they are there in front of him, as if he is thumbing through them as he speaks—*The photographs are from our war*, he says, *and they are very, very disturbing.*

My first semester of teaching in Houston has just ended, and I'm driving north, headed back to New York, where both Anna and Inez live. At this point Anna and I are already involved—Inez and I have yet to meet. I'm driving a 1993 Ford Escort wagon—reliable, unsexy, cheap—a basic a-to-b device, bought in Texas with the idea of taking it north because, unlike in the northeast, a used car from Texas will be unlikely to have rust. You just have to make sure it was never in a flood. Houston, built on a swamp, is known for its floods. Houston, also, is seemingly endless—I hear about the photographs again and again even before I make it to the city limits. What connects the photographs, the man on the radio says, is that each depicts what appears to be torture, and that the people doing the torturing are wearing uniforms, or parts of uniforms, and that the uniforms appear to be ours. The man on the radio describes the photographs—prisoners, guards, dogs. Hallways, cinderblocks, cages. Leashes. Smiles. *Many of the prisoners are not wearing clothes,* he says. *The reason for this,* he says, *is that there appears to be a sexual element to what's happening,* as I float past a church the size of a shopping mall.

The man on the radio is a reporter. The first time I heard his name was nearly forty years ago, when he broke the story of a massacre in Vietnam—My Lai—the name of a hamlet that came to symbolize all that was wrong with that war. Nearly four hundred unarmed men, women, and children—civilians—rounded up, executed, many of them herded into ditches and shot. Photographs document that day as well, and the photographs made their way to his hands, and eventually to the pages of the *New York Times.* WELCOME TO THE YEAR OF THE MONKEY, banners over the streets of Saigon read that spring of 1968.

I finally break out of the vortex that is Houston, and now I'm heading east on I-10, approaching the exit for New Orleans, where I'd planned to stop—I haven't been there for years—but I decide to push on, to make it to Tuscaloosa before nightfall, where friends have offered shelter. And I never get to see New Orleans again.

two

they came back

(2007) That time of year again—short days, long nights— almost Christmas, but first comes the anniversary of my mother's death, a nail in the middle of the snow. *Happy Deathday*, I say, though the room is empty. Every year around this time I'm filled with a dark energy, so I watch zombie movies, and if you were to see a photograph of me from one of those nights you might think I was a zombie myself. Hold up one hand, that's how many days I have until the deathday passes, that's how many more zombie movies I can watch. *Hiroshima Mon Amour. After Life. American Psycho.* In *Dawn of the Dead* the zombies return to the mall, like those eerie photographs the newspapers run every year at this time, the poor lined up outside a Wal-Mart, waiting for the sale to begin. In last night's feature a father became a zombie and spent the rest of the movie chasing his children through the empty London streets—he had told them their mother was dead but she was not dead. Tonight I chose a French one—*They Came Back*—subtle, I think, for the genre: the only thing the dead do is act dead, shuffling listlessly to work and back. They do not want our blood, or our brains, to keep going. They seem unsure if they even want to keep going.

~

Night of the Living Dead was my first zombie movie. My mother took my brother and me—I was ten. For months afterward we'd reenact our favorite scenes in the kitchen, shuffling up behind each other, arms dangling lifelessly by our sides, or scratching at the screen door, our eyes never blinking. At dinner I'd put a life-sized severed rubber hand on my plate, drizzle it with fake blood, stab at it with my fork. My father had been gone since I was six months old—he wasn't even a distant memory at this point. My mother was still young, not even thirty. Over the years she'd had a series of boyfriends, decent enough guys, at least the ones she brought home. One of them, a year or so after our *Night of the Living Dead*, would take me to the drive-in to see zombie and mayhem movies—*Bloody Mama, Scream and Scream Again*. That Christmas he gave me a book on the history of torture. The font used for the title, as I remember it, was Old English, the type of lettering now used by heavy metal bands and for A.A. slogans—*One Day at a Time. Motörhead*.

~

(1999) For a few years after my mother died, I found it best to simply disappear for the whole of December—Muslim countries were best, where I wouldn't be tormented by Christmas carols. I had a friend working in Cairo, so one winter I fled there to escape the cold of New York and a failing relationship. My second morning there I woke up next to a woman I would eventually fall in love with, but she lived in Copenhagen and I lived in New York and we were both with other people and perhaps neither of us was ready to be in love. Jetlagged, we took a walk to an enormous cemetery that had become a city for the

dispossessed. Families lived in the crypts, and no one knew if it was their dead they were mourning, or merely an empty crypt. This city of squatters, this zombie city, had been there so long that some of the crypts had become shops, and the passageways had lights strung up along them. When we got to the edge of it, we crossed a highway to an area that was simply white on our map. It was dusk. At an outdoor stand we bought an entire fried fish, and ate it as we walked. At one point, in an alley, some children began to follow us, and they began to swing long thin sticks in the air, which cracked near our faces. I knew the phrase "Go away" in Arabic, which I'd already used on occasion with beggars, feeling miserable each time. *Go away*, I hissed, and stamped my feet, and grabbed one of their switches, and tossed it over a fence. *Go away*.

~

(*2003*) After two years in Rome, where I'd finished the book on homelessness and my father, I made my way back to Brooklyn. While I'd been away, the building I'd lived in for ten years had been bought by the artists who'd lived below me, and they'd quadrupled the rent. I had some money left from my book advance, enough to either rent a place in Brooklyn for a year, or buy a house upstate. I bought the house, a rundown Victorian in a pretty village on the Hudson River, two hours north of the city. Rip Van Winkle country—my neighbors really had seemed to have fallen asleep for twenty years. I closed in December.

At this point the relationship with the Italian playwright wasn't going very well. We had plans for her to join me once I settled in, but it often seemed she was angry with me, some days for not being able to promise I'd meet her in eternity. I accepted that this was how she interpreted her Catholicism, but it worried me. A few months earlier, by chance, I'd been commissioned to write a one-act play—no big deal, but I figured I could learn something from the process. On the anniversary of my mother's death, the playwright told me, by phone, that she'd rather see me kill myself than write a play. Apparently she felt threatened. I'd been trying to reassure her, but with her words—*I'd rather see you kill yourself*—I knew the relationship was over. I hung up the phone. Then, looking around me, perched on a salvaged couch in a trashy house in a town that time forgot, I wondered what I'd done. Had I really poured all my money into something that would take years to bring back to life? Maybe I could simply fall asleep in it, never wake up.

What I couldn't know then was that Inez lived a few miles down the road.

~

(2007) In a dream last night Inez was walking away from me, through a prisonlike complex. A guard stopped me, said I couldn't follow her. I watched on a video monitor as she walked down a hall, took a right, and then I lost sight of her. The guard had a dog, and it pinned me to a table, and this was how the dream ended. I woke up from the dream in a white room in Brooklyn, the apartment Inez and I moved into two months ago (surprisingly, this is the first time that I have ever lived with a woman). Inez is asleep beside me, this is our bedroom. When she opened her eyes, I closed mine, so I could tell her the dream. It also involved driving a car very close to the edge of a cliff.

Our baby is due in a month.

Last week the Danish woman sent me a photograph of herself, very pregnant. Yesterday, I ran into another lover from the past, but I confused her with her twin sister. Years ago, when I came back from Egypt, I went back to Brooklyn, to my failing relationship with Justine, but she looked at me like the woman in the French zombie movie, when her lover returns from the dead. *You came back*, she looked like she wanted to say, but we both knew I hadn't, not really. In fact, now, when we meet up, years later, it's to talk about how badly I'd handled everything. *Do you know how hard it was for me then? I woke up next to the man I loved and he'd transformed into a psychotic killer.*

Just a zombie, I want to say.

who died and made you king?

(1974) If, without taking your eyes from the television, you call out for a glass of water and your mother, stirring some onions in a pan, answers, *Who died and made you king?*—it might make you wonder if you were, in fact, a king. Unknown, unrecognized, but still—a king. Or, if you call out for a glass of water and your mother, as she passes on her way out, answers, *Who was your slave yesterday?*—it might mean something else. Or it might mean the same thing, for kings, after all, often have slaves, the two often go together, you know this.

In school you study the Civil Rights movement, but you aren't interested in civil rights. You're interested in the Middle Ages, a time of kings and dungeons, which they don't teach in school. *Medieval*, you like to say the word, it has the word "evil" in it. Today the teacher is talking about Martin Luther King— every year you learn the same four things about Martin Luther King—but you are thinking about Nebuchadnezzar, the king of ancient Babylon. God took away his kingdom in order to punish him for his pride, and then God condemned him to live in the woods like an animal. God, apparently, doesn't like one to have pride. For seven years Nebuchadnezzar lived without society or the ability to think. Hair grew all over his body, his nails became claws.

You look at your own hand, stretch your fingers out.

Martin Luther King sat in a Birmingham jail, locked up for supporting the right for a man to order a sandwich whenever and wherever he damn well pleased. Your father is in prison, your mother told you so, the prison is in Missouri, but that's all you've heard. From the big map on the wall, the one you stare at when you're supposed to be listening, you know Missouri is in the middle of nowhere. The teacher says that while in prison Martin Luther King wrote a letter. You were supposed to read the letter for homework. *Can anyone tell us one thing he wrote in his letter?* She looks straight at you as she says this—you blur your eyes and she dissolves.

Back home, belly-down on the floor, you read the funnies while your mother reads the obituaries. You look for *The Wizard of Id*—you like Spook, the troll-like guy, chained up forever in that dungeon. You like how every time Spook appears he tries to escape, and you both want him to make it and want him to be there the next time you visit.

One day your mother passes on a letter your father has sent you from prison. In the envelope, along with the one-page letter, he has included a clipping from the newspaper—*The Wizard of Id*. Spook is chained to a wall, a hooded man holding a whip stands behind him.

If you ask your mother why your father is in prison she might say, *Your father is a reprobate.* Since you don't know what a reprobate is, you might think it's a type of king.

But it's more likely that you'll think it's a type of spook.

Your father, from what you remember, from the one time you remember meeting him, looks like a cross between Andy Williams and the Cowardly Lion. All of your mother's boyfriends remind you of someone you've seen on tv. Tom Jones. Dick Cavett. Gregg Allman.

One day you will learn that what was once Babylon is now Iraq. Years later, after your country invades, its king, its president, will be found, some months later, hiding in what will be called "a spider hole"—his beard gone wild, his nails grown long. And some days after this, after he is sentenced to death, he will be hung by the neck by jeering hooded men. You will watch his execution on the same day you see a photograph of a lost pop star showing her pussy to the world.

But for now it is still that beautiful spring day, and you are still inside. Your mother hasn't gone out yet. Tonight she'll bartend until two, but she doesn't have to go in until dark—anything could still happen. The two of you could head down to the harbor, get some ice cream, park by Peggotty Beach, watch the summer people try to swim in the still-cold Atlantic. You could help her chop carrots and onions for her chicken stew. You could drive around the cliffs, past all the big houses teetering on the edge of the ocean, make bets on which will be pulled in next. But if she's going out to meet her latest boyfriend, the cop (Elvis), it wouldn't make sense for you to go with her. What would you do, play with his gun again while they make out in the front seat? As she passes you on her way out, you are still belly-down, now staring into your box of shadows—*The Three Stooges* now, Curly's head in a vice again, Moe cutting into it with a hacksaw. Moe, it seems, is forever trying to carve his way into someone else's body.

one simple question

(1995) I'm working as an itinerant poet in New York City Public Schools—Harlem, the South Bronx, Crown Heights—reading poems to young people, helping them to write their own. These are the years of unprecedented wealth in the United States, and if you want to find the worst public school in any city you just have to look up the one named after Martin Luther King. The schools I work in are in neighborhoods that look like Dresden after the firebombing, though the carpetbaggers, the speculators, are already making inroads, buying up the burned-out shells. To start a class I sometimes read the poem *A Story That Could Be True* by William Stafford. It deals, in part, with a missing father, and I know that the fathers of many of these kids are missing. The poem starts:

> If you were exchanged in the cradle and
> your real mother died
> without ever telling the story
> then no one knows your name,
> and somewhere in the world
> your father is lost and needs you
> but you are far away.

I'd choke up every time I'd read it outloud, for reasons that were mysterious to me then but seem obvious now. For six years my father had lived like Nebuchadnezzar, without society or the ability to think—hair grew all over his body, his nails became claws.

> He can never find
> how true you are, how ready.
> When the great wind comes
> and the robberies of the rain
> you stand on the corner shivering.
> The people who go by—
> you wonder at their calm.

By the time I was reading Stafford to second-graders in Harlem, my father had been off the streets for nearly five years, living in his government-subsidized studio apartment in downtown Boston. But once again I'd lost contact with him, once again he'd slipped into the shadows. Or I had. When I found him again, I told myself I wanted to ask him just one simple question—how had he met my mother?—but I had to keep going back, for it took years for him to answer this question.

as we drive slowly past
the burning house

(1971) When a siren—police car or fire truck or ambulance—
punctured my Saturday morning cartoons, twisting the blue
from the sky, my mother would tell me to go start the car.
Let's see what's happening, she'd say, and we'd drive, to the place
where the sirens called us. Afterward we'd drive to the coffee
shop in the harbor and I'd go in and order her the usual—*cream
no sugar*—while she'd wait in the car. She'd worked in that same
coffee shop when she was in high school—it was where she met
my father. *I don't want to give them anything more to talk about,*
she'd once told me, to explain why she'd send me in alone.

After I'd come back with her coffee, we'd drive to the beach,
sit in the car, look out at the Atlantic. One day she told me that
she was thinking of marrying a carpenter she'd been seeing for
a couple months. *Travis wants me to marry him,* she said. *What
do you think?* Travis was just back from Vietnam—ten years
younger than her, ten years older than me (I'm eleven)—a nice
enough guy, but a little wild.

That's a mistake, I tell her.

A couple weeks later Travis is living in our house.

After they're married, my mother and I still drive toward
our burning houses. Travis never joins us—maybe he's never

invited. Once we drove past the house of a woman who'd killed herself—no siren had announced it. Maybe we read about it in the paper, maybe we heard about it from a neighbor, but still we got in the car, and drove slowly past. It was a house I'd never noticed, though I'd passed by it every morning on my paper route, the windows now curtained shut, the grass already overgrown.

scylla

As we drove past our burning houses, what was my mother hoping to find, what was she hoping I'd see? Was she hoping to teach me to pay close attention to the world. Or to pay close attention to the afterworld? In *The Odyssey* the Sirens sang out to Odysseus to lull him into stranding his ship on the shoals— it could be argued that our sirens were merely calling out to strand us as well, to scuttle our ship, only it would take years to know that was what they were doing. Or, it could be argued, at least it wasn't our tragedy, at least we were able to step outside our house for an hour, into the fresh air, to witness something outside ourselves. To empathize, or to practice empathy, even though we never knew the people who'd lived in the burning houses, nor did it seem we cared to, even after their house was gone. What could we have possibly offered—a room in our falling-down house? (*There was no room*) A meal, a blanket, some clothes? (*We never did*)

Or maybe my mother simply wanted me to practice, like other families practiced fire drills, so that when the sirens came for her I'd know what to do. To get in the car and drive, toward the sound, whatever it was—fire or heart attack, car crash or suicide—to get out and stand on the sidewalk or on someone's lawn. Or to not even stop, to make it a slow drive-by, while the stranger is carried away on a stretcher. But where do you drive to when the siren is outside your own house? What do you look at when the strangers on the sidewalk are looking at you?

you don't take pictures

(2004) On the day the photographs appear, a veteran of the Korean War is interviewed on the radio in a coffee shop in Tennessee. By now the photographs are in every newspaper in the world, it sounds as if he is thumbing through them as he speaks. *You know*, he begins slowly, searching for the words— *stuff like this happens in every war.* It's hard to tell if he's disgusted or merely baffled. He pauses, then his voice gets slightly more indignant—*but you don't take pictures.*

The next day a radio commentator weighs in—*This is no different than what happens at the Skull and Bones initiation. And we're going to ruin people's lives over it and we're going to hamper our military effort, and then we're going to really hammer them because they had a good time. You know, these people are being fired at every day. I'm talking about people having a good time. These people, you ever heard of emotional release? You heard of the need to blow some steam off?* This is the moment before the soldiers dragging prisoners on leashes and giving the thumbs-up behind pyramids of naked men will come to be known as *a few bad apples.* This is the moment when the soldiers are just like us, which—strangely, uncomfortably—is perhaps closer to the truth.

~

(1984) While living in Boston, when I was still drinking, I began working in a homeless shelter. I was twenty-four years old, my father had yet to be evicted, and I had no way of knowing what was to come. Sometimes, on weekends, I was named "supervisor," put in charge of other workers—some were twenty-two, some were fifty-two. At our change-of-shift meetings we'd vote on whether to bar this guy or that one, to put him out for a day, or a year, thumbs up, thumbs down. Afterward, when these barrees came to the door, hoping to be let in for the night, we'd stop them, turn them around, send them back out into the snowy darkness. We knew they could die out there, but (lord of the flies) we'd been given the power of life and death. I'd step over bodies on my way home from work each morning, and sometimes I'd watch children, on their way to school, step over the same bodies. They held on to their mother's hand, and I'd hear them ask, Why's that man asleep on the sidewalk? Twenty years later, and some of those same children volunteered to go to Iraq. Maybe they thought they could do some good, maybe they thought they might even save someone, or a city, or the world. Or maybe they just wanted to come back and be able to afford college. But that's not why they were sent. Maybe it isn't so hard to get someone who has grown up with the idea that human beings are disposable to brutalize someone else—especially someone who doesn't look like them, or speak their language, or worship their god—even if all they want to do (was it possible they were there and not haunted?) is help.

~

A few days after the photographs are leaked to the world, at a press conference on what is beginning to be called a "scandal," the secretary of defense says, *I don't know if it is correct to say what you just said that torture has taken place, or that there's been a conviction for torture. And therefore I'm not going to address the torture word.* The torture word. A few days later a U.S. senator will echo the pronouncement that the photographs show little more than what goes on at a fraternity hazing. Charles Krauthammer (I'm not really sure what Krauthammer, with his comic-book bad-guy name, actually does for a living) will be more explicit—*we must all be prepared to torture.*

thrown it all away

(1987) I'd been working in a homeless shelter for three years (a
lifetime) when my father got himself evicted from his low-rent
apartment, a ten-minute walk from my own low-rent apartment, in downtown Boston. We lived that close to each other,
yet until he got evicted our paths had never crossed. After the
eviction he lived for a few years on the streets, and some nights,
many nights, he slept in the shelter where I worked, which sent
me into a tailspin, at first, but eventually got me into therapy,
and sober. My tailspin, truth be told, was merely the accelera-
tion of an ongoing, if mundane, tale of liquor and drugs and
late nights with women who weren't always my girlfriend. By
the time I was working with the homeless, I'd been arrested a
few times, spent a few hours in protective custody, totaled a few
vehicles, lied a few times to this girlfriend or that. By the time I
was working with the homeless, even I could see that I'd rarely
been arrested, or left, when I didn't deserve it. I knew that the
cop, or girlfriend, had likely saved my life more than once, by
simply towing away my car, or by simply saying *enough*.

In the shelter I got to know a few cops, the duty officers hired
to work security. Outside the shelter, I'd see them at the pro-
tests we'd organize, at the tent cities we set up, or at the aban-

doned government-owned buildings we tore the boards off of and occupied, demanding they be renovated into low-income housing. At one demonstration one of these same cops arrested me, and he smiled as he put the cuffs on me. A hard-ass, a ball-buster, like most cops—it seemed I shouldn't like him, but I did. He was like those lumberjacks I got to know a few years later on Meares Island, home of one of the last old-growth forests in North America, in the Clayoquot Sound, a system of waterways on the west coast of Vancouver Island. These lumberjacks sat on a bridge with us, the protesters, while the Mounties tried to extract our friend from the log she'd chained herself to— we'd rolled the log in place the night before to block the logging trucks from crossing the bridge. It was slow going, as our friend was straddling one end of the log, which jutted out over the edge of the bridge, dangling her over the river, far below. If they jarred her, she could fall, which wouldn't make for good headlines, for either the Mounties or the lumber industry. This action slowed their trucks down for a day, and in that day we found out that the lumberjacks were really no different from us, just trying to get through another day. They reminded me of my mother's boyfriends when I was growing up—the carpenter and the gangster, the fisherman and the guy who ran the Concrete Pipe Corporation—guys I got to know and like. None of them were much different from the guys who were building the nuclear power plant just over the state line in New Hampshire. I worked in that town for a couple weeks one summer, building greenhouses. At lunchtime, in the sandwich shops, I'd see the nuke plant guys—they didn't look that much different from me. Later, when I was in college, friends I knew would go back to that town to protest the plant. A few years later

I read that there were problems with it, structural problems—it came out that the workers had been filmed getting high in their cars in the parking lots at lunchtime, so all these problems were blamed on them. It was the late seventies, then it was the early eighties. Everyone was high—the guys who built the nuclear power plant, the kids who went up to protest it, my father as he entered his first bank, my mother as she loaded her gun, me as I stood before her coffin, as I reached out to touch her cheek, murmuring to my brother, *She's not even real.* It was how we made it through our days, wrapped in gauze, frozen, like Walt Disney, waiting for some scientific discovery that would make it possible to wake up again, one day.

I'll try to say this in another way:

(*1977*) I'm riding shotgun in my friend Phil's oversized Impala, listening to the Cars on an 8-track—*Since you're gone, I took the big vacation.* My mother, in her late thirties, works as a waitress weekend nights, after her day job at the bank, serving up fish-and-chips and bottled beer as the locals listen to the bar band. The bar band for a couple years, up until the moment their first album will make them famous, is the Cars.

I can't help it, when you fall apart.

By now I know she's going, not like I know everyone's going, eventually, but with an unease I've carried since birth. Part of me imagines she'll just up and leave, drive off with a guy she met at the bar, and she probably did, more than once. More than once she didn't make it home, nights my brother and I stayed at our grandmother's. It's not that she hadn't warned me, she'd told me she wouldn't be around forever, told me where the important papers were—the documents, the instructions.

Instructions? When the time came, the instructions meant nothing—doggerel, gibberish, babble (*well, nothing's making sense*)—when the time came, the money meant nothing. All I wanted was a few crumbs to lead me back, all I want is to ask her one question, one small question.

three

a box of dolls

(2007) I have been on this train, heading south along this river, the river off to my right, forever, it seems. I can't complain. I got on early, got a window, and if I want I can look up and see the river and whatever is washed up along its banks and the little fallen houses that I still imagine I will one day wander through—like that one, the door left open, as if someone went out for a look at the river on a day like this, a warm fall day, and simply never came back.

~

Two months before our daughter is born, Inez and I go to an infant CPR class. I have taken CPR classes before, but never specifically to save an infant. The woman leading it is passionate about safety, pumping us with gruesome details of what could happen if we fail to put our child in a secured car seat, if she swallows a penny, if we spill hot coffee on her. *One day you will come upon your baby and she will be blue*, this woman says. *What will you do?* A box of dolls at her feet, dolls with removable rubber faces, and chests that can be compressed only if the air passage is opened. As she speaks she wraps a face around a skull and assures us that each has been sterilized since the last class. *I take them home and boil them*, she says. She places a doll face-up on the table in front of each of us, along with a packet of alcohol, so we can give the doll's mouth one last wipe before we attempt to revive her. By the looks on everyone's face we are all a little freaked out (or maybe it's just me). *Take two fingers*, the teacher says, *place them just below your baby's nipples, in the center of her chest, and push.*

~

I cannot imagine my mother and father in a room like this, trying to revive a doll. Were there even classes back then for expecting parents? I get the idea that when they were young pregnancy simply was, a state one dealt with, or not. I heard from my father, more than once, that my mother, at seventeen, pregnant with my brother, had considered having an abortion. I heard from one of her ex-boyfriends that, two years later, pregnant with me, she'd attempted suicide, or maybe it was right after I was born, and that—obviously—she'd failed. Or maybe she'd turned away from it in time. I don't know if any of this is true, and there's no longer any way to know. About the suicide attempt, I've only heard it once, and the source, this ex-boyfriend, seemed bitter, reluctant to talk, maybe even a bit paranoid. He was the first boyfriend I remember my mother being with. They were together nearly five years, though he claimed it was only two. Part of that time he was also living with his wife, and they had three kids of their own, so maybe he doesn't count those early years. He and his wife eventually divorced, and, being Catholic, it wore on his soul. Years later, by the time I found him again, he could only mutter that it had all been a mistake. As for my mother's early suicide attempt, if true it wouldn't surprise me. It often felt like my brother and I—her kids—were tethering her to this world, while at the same time the burden of raising us alone was pulling her under.

the book of daniel

In one early scene in E. L. Doctorow's *The Book of Daniel*, the eponymous main character, a fictionalized version of one of the children left behind when the Rosenbergs were executed, is driving back to his family home with his girlfriend. Nothing is said, they are not speaking, but since we have access to his thoughts we know he is full of rage. At some point he lets her know, somehow, what he wants, and, sobbing quietly, their child asleep in the backseat, she agrees. She kneels on the seat, pulls up her skirt, pulls down her underwear, and offers up her bared ass to him. He strokes it briefly, as if he might push his fingers into her, but instead he pushes in the cigarette lighter, and when it pops out he takes it and burns her with it as he steers with his other hand.

~

(2004) A few days after the Abu Ghraib photographs appear, I pull into New York in the car I'd driven up from Texas, and I make my way to Anna. I tell her that I am in no shape to see anyone, not fully, that I will likely see others, though this will not stop me from going to her whenever I make my way to Brooklyn. And so, over the weeks, we grow closer, but at some

point I meet someone else—Inez—though I am still not ready to be with anyone, not really, not fully. At first I tell Inez about Anna, and then I let each assume that I've stopped seeing the other, until I wake up that day in Texas, a year later, in love with two women, honest with neither, and in as dark a place as I've been in a long, long time—*In the middle of my life I found myself in a deep dark wood, having lost the way.* When I was with one, I dreaded a call from the other, so my phone was always silenced, when I spoke I used the name *sweetie* or *honey* or *darling* so as not to make a mistake. I'd spent the years since I'd quit drinking practicing being honest, and it stunned me how quickly that dissolved, how easily one lie folded into the next, how I could be on my cellphone telling one (which one?) that I was about to go to bed when in fact at that moment I was driving to Austin. Until I began to hear a voice in my head, I can't pinpoint precisely when it started, quiet at first, comforting, murmuring, that if I was dead then the mess I'd gotten myself into would be lifted, the damage I was spreading would be made right.

One night I tell Anna that I feel like Daniel in Doctorow's book. I tell her about the cigarette lighter, how he tries to make her feel the pain he feels. I tell her this as a warning. I wasn't offering or asking to burn her, it's just I was having trouble committing—to her, to anything—and I was having a hard time articulating why.

god's loneliness (known)

Soon—very soon—I shall be known: these are the first words my father, locked up for robbing banks, or something like robbing banks, wrote me. His return address was #9567328, Federal Prison, Springfield, Missouri. I often hear myself calling him a bankrobber, perhaps because the word "bankrobber" has more electricity in it than "fuckup." His charge was "interstate transportation of stolen securities"—he'd entered a few banks and said a few words and passed a few bad checks and left with money that wasn't his. In every bank he'd been photographed, smiling into the camera. *Soon—very soon—I shall be known.* Known? What else did anyone need to know?

According to some Sufis, it was God's loneliness and desire to be known that set creation going. When I was still drinking, though maybe not enjoying it as much as I once had (*first the man takes a drink, then the drink takes a drink, then the drink takes the man*), a lover turned to me, her palm flat on my chest—*You know*, she said, *I don't really know you at all.* We'd been together for a few months, likely she was simply expressing a desire to get to know me better, to get invited inside the walls of my invisible fortress, the one I'd been building my whole life.

The thing was, the whole point, was that no one was invited in. I might refer to this or that rough patch from my little box of tragedies, hold them up likes slides to a lightbulb—*proof*—but that was just to get whoever was listening to hold on to me a little tighter. It had nothing to do with them getting inside. Inside this fortress a man was wrestling with his own shadow, muttering that he'd never let himself be surprised, not again. Muttering that he'd never again let himself be tricked into getting so close to someone that he might risk missing her.

God's loneliness and desire to be known set creation going. Unmanifest things, lacking names, remained unmanifest until the violence of God's sense of isolation sent the heavens into a spasm of procreating words that then became matter.

The violence of God's sense of isolation.

Another lover, shortly after I quit drinking, told me that my eyes were dead. Maybe they were, but her saying it pierced that wall again, and at the time I still wasn't ready for it to be disturbed. She was German, and so I forgave her bluntness (*Your ears taste like poison*, she'd murmur as we'd kiss). This was just days before the Berlin Wall came down, and when it did she flew home. A few months later I showed up at her door in Kreutzberg, something we'd talked about since our teary good-bye (*You're coming out of me now*, she'd whispered at the airport, pulling my hand back to her crotch), but by then she was living with someone else.

the allegory of the cave

My mother, the story goes, set our house on fire one summer night. The house was a ruin, she did it to collect the insurance money, so she could then have it fixed up, *re-no-vated* (a big word, like *re-pro-bate*). I was five, my brother and I were sleeping upstairs at the time. I remember being carried outside in my ghoulish pajamas, left to stand across the street on the lawn of the neighbor we'd never met. I stood there, watching our house burn, then I watched the shadows of it burning, like one of those prisoners in Plato's cave. It was only years later that I learned my mother set it, or was told she set it, by the boyfriend she was with at the time (the same boyfriend who told me she'd attempted suicide before, or shortly after, I was born). It made sense, when I heard it, though it doesn't mean it's true—not that our house caught fire, but that she set it. If true, then it might explain why thereafter we were fated to go toward sirens, it might answer the question of why every burning house pulled us toward it—maybe she believed she could tell by looking everyone in the eye as they came out of the house if it was a scam or not. Or maybe she just wanted to make sure all the children made it out okay.

~

The Allegory of the Cave came from a dream Plato had. In this dream prisoners, locked-up in a cave since childhood, are chained in such a way that they cannot look away from the wall they are facing. Even their heads are fixed, somehow, in that one direction. Behind the prisoners, some still children, is a walkway, slightly elevated, and along this walkway the jailers, or their assistants, carry various objects back and forth. Beyond the walkway a fire burns, continuously, a large fire, and this fire casts light onto the objects, which then cast shadows on the wall for the prisoners to contemplate. The object might be something benign, a bunch of carrots, say, but as a shadow the carrots can appear frightful—each could be a knife. Or an apple could be a rock that could crush a man's hands. Or his son's testicles. Or a jar of milk could be a jar of acid, if all one sees, all one is allowed to see, are shadows. And the jailers grunt and snort, sounds that echo off the walls and so seem, to the prisoners, to come from the shadows themselves. And don't forget the fire, which makes another sound, and which heats their backs, perhaps too much, and fills the cave with smoke, making it hard to breathe. It must seem a little like hell, with its silent goons carrying menacing shapes, with your head strapped into place, though this allegory comes from a time well before we perfected our modern-day concept of hell.

~

(*2001*) A few days after the towers fall, the vice president (the second-in-command, who some claim is the first-in-command), goes on television to make a pronouncement—*We also have to work, though, sort of the dark side, if you will. . . . it's going to be vital for us to use any means at our disposal, basically, to achieve our objective.*

A few weeks after the vice president invites us over to the dark side, a man named Ibn al-Shaykh al-Libi is flown by the United States, via a secret program called "extraordinary rendition" (a euphemism for "state-sponsored kidnapping" or "outsourcing torture"), to a dungeon in Egypt, where he will utter a lie about chemical weapons and Saddam and Osama, a lie extracted under torture, a lie that will later be used to justify a war. A year later the secretary of state, who is believed by most, until this moment, to embody an above-average amount of integrity, will repeat this lie. He will repeat it at the U.N., on a world stage, the lie that he has the evidence, and the evidence is strong, that Osama passed chemical weapons on to Saddam, and that Saddam has the missiles to strike Europe with these weapons in fifteen minutes. The secretary of state, in an unusual moment of theater, will even hold up a small vial of a white powder, and say that if it were anthrax it would be enough to kill all of London—which is true, if it were anthrax, but this is a potential truth buried in a tangible lie. Most will believe him when he says that U.N. inspections haven't worked, that there is an urgency to act. I will believe him, for a moment, until a document, folded into the same lie, referring to the purchase of something quaintly called "yellowcake," reveals itself to be a clumsy forgery. Only later will it be revealed that the original lie, the one that connected Osama and Saddam, the one that led us into our long war, was extracted by torture.

~

If Plato had seen me standing outside my burning house in my ghoulish pajamas that summer night, hypnotized by shadows, what would he have said? What would he have written if he had seen me transfixed by the Three Stooges, pummeling each other day after day? What insight would he have had if he saw me standing in a Best Buy on Broadway before a whole bank of televisions, watching the first tower fall, when I could have simply looked south and seen the real thing? Would he say I was caught up in the world as it appeared, unable to enter into its essence? Would he say my eyes were having trouble adjusting to the light? *The Allegory of the Cave* is often read as an allegory of perception, how we come to believe that the shadows on the wall, which terrify or entertain us, are real. But how did we end up in a cave, how did we end up, hour after hour, day after day, staring at shadows on the wall. And why don't we simply look away?

john doe

Some mornings you wake up fully in your body, and you know this is all there is—the air, the shape your body makes in the air, your hand, the skin that covers your hand, the air that covers your skin, the light that fills the air, a few colors in the light, this one thought, this dream dissolving—it is a dream that, in your half-awake state, embarrasses you. You don't tell it to the woman waking up beside you, the woman you love, because it is about another woman, whom you might also love. This is the dream you need to hold on to, this is your shadow speaking, attempting to bewilder you again. Sometimes, if you lay still, you can feel the air entering each cell, sometimes you can feel the blood in your lips. Sometimes, if you lay very still, you can feel the whole web tremble.

~

(1988) Early December, and I'm working the Homeless Outreach Van with a woman I'll call Kate. Kate's a rookie, tonight is her first time out on the Van. I haven't been in charge of the Van before, but I am tonight. It's not quite freezing, but cold, touching forty. It's also the anniversary of my mother's death,

six years earlier, and that dark energy is roiling through me.
My father has been homeless for almost two years by this point,
and it is impossible for me not to be aware that he looms ahead,
somewhere in the night, his body curled up somewhere, breathing, or not.

A couple hours into it we drive past a man on a bench at
the edge of Boston Common. A black man in his forties, a man
I've never seen before, wild-eyed and skittish, his jacket on the
ground beside him. We pull up, get out, approach. He looks at
us, tries to speak, his tongue thick, slurred—he is, seemingly,
completely shattered. *Amigo*, I say, *how about we go to the shelter, it's too frikkin cold to hang out here.* He shakes his head, or
his head lolls, utters something unintelligible. Kate and I look
at each other. If Jeff were here, maybe we'd just grab the guy
and throw him in the Van, *shanghai* him, though it's risky. The
Van, after all, is a small, enclosed space, no cage separating the
driver from the drunk. He could start using his hands, he could
start swinging, it could be a nightmare. Kate and I stand beside
each other, our breath steams out of us. I decide to try anyway,
I tell Kate the plan. She looks doubtful, but we get on either side
of him, murmuring like he's an infant or a cat, *Okay, here we go,
nice and warm inside, we're going to take you to a better place, let you
sleep it off, in the morning it will all be a bad dream, upsy-daisy, here
we go*—but he starts to flail, swinging his head back and forth,
he pulls away from us, slides from our hands into a pile on the
ground, his shirt now pulled up over his chest. Great—now
he's in even worse shape than when we found him, lying on the
asphalt, his bared skin exposed, still flailing. We kneel down,
try to keep him from whacking his head, hoist him back up to

the bench, step away. I send Kate to get a couple blankets, apologize for our manhandling, assure him that we're the good guys. Not one word that comes out of his mouth is comprehensible. One of the talking comatose, a walking blackout. We wrap the blankets around his shoulders and he struggles against them, like they're sandpaper. Kate and I look at each other, uncertain. It's a cold night, a lot of other people to see. We tell him we'll be back in half an hour to check on how he's doing, and as we drive away, the blankets slide to the ground.

An hour later Kate reminds me we should check on our John Doe, before we leave Downtown Crossing. He'd completely left my radar, overtaken by the dozen or so others we'd subsequently encountered. Overtaken by how well Kate and I are getting along. I'm due to see a therapist for the first time the next day, and I've told her about my upcoming appointment. As we drive back past Park Street Station, we see him, now flat out on the ground, the blankets nowhere near. I park beside him, get out, shake his shoulder, wait for him to mumble incoherently, to flail. Nothing. Unresponsive. I try rubbing my knuckles across his sternum, try digging a pen cap into his thumbnail. Nothing. I suddenly realize that I have no idea what I'm doing. I try to find a pulse, dig my fingers into his neck, like I've seen on tv. A bare, distant pulse, or maybe nothing, I don't know, can't tell for sure. I tell Kate to call 911, man down, not breathing. This is before the invention of cellphones, what we have is a little radio that connects us to the front desk at the shelter, and then they call 911. I don't even know CPR, or if I do I can't remember where to begin, though with even a minimal pulse I don't think I'm supposed to begin. But do I know that for sure? An ambulance is there in minutes, amazingly, and the EMTs jump out, ask how long he's been down. They check his pulse, immediately cut his shirt off so his chest is now exposed to the night. One already has the black box of electricity out and is uncoiling its wires. One rubs goo on John Doe's chest while the other rubs the two little irons together (*like a fly washing its hands*, I think). Then the one with the irons shouts *Clear*, just like on tv, pressing the irons into John Doe's ribs so his body lifts off the ground as if he's been kicked—*clear clear clear*—an ear to the chest between each. Then nothing more. They strap him to a gurney and toss it into the back of their van and speed off, leaving Kate and me looking down at the blankets we'd placed over his shoulders an hour before.

The next morning I go to the morgue with Joy, who's worked at the shelter for years, who knows everyone, but even to Joy he's John Doe.

~

The day after John Doe dies, after my trip to the morgue, I meet with the therapist. The appointment was set up weeks earlier. It's just a coincidence that someone died on me a few hours earlier, and that it's the anniversary of my mother's suicide. As part of my intake the therapist asks me what's going on, why I am there. I tell him about the anniversary, I tell him that my father is going on two years homeless, that my friend and roommate Richard was diagnosed HIV positive a year before, that everyone in my building is a junkie, that my ten-year relationship is nearing the end, and now John Fucken Doe, alive one minute and dead the next—I spoke to him, made a decision, drove away. I leaned in toward Kate, and thereby away from him.

The therapist smiles, shakes his head, asks if I think he's a miracle worker. I smile. A few days later I find out that hypothermia, in its extreme form, mimics drunkenness.

worksong

Here, God says, here is your cupful of days.

If you don't believe in God, you still get your cupful of days. Some will be spent making love, some will be spent high, some will be spent reading *Ulysses*, and some will be spent alone. Some will be spent around a table, a meal about to be passed, a steaming bowl of rice, some sautéed kale. It's someone's birthday, someone you have known for ten, no, twenty, years. To your right is a woman you slept with seven years ago—at the time, you thought it might work out, but it didn't. Across from you is the woman you are with now, and at this point it could be forever, whatever that means.

Some of the days you are given will be spent in a strange city, and at the end of the day you will know that you have spoken to no one except the girl you got your coffee from, no one except her. There will always be days like this.

horror vacui

(1988) After John Doe died, the higher-ups in the shelter decided
we all needed CPR training. They also offered a "Death and
Dying Workshop," though this was optional. What I remember
of the workshop was that at some point the facilitator had us
write out a list of the ten most important things in our lives.
This list could include people, objects, things we liked to do, a
memory that was important to us. She gave us a few minutes
to make our list, and then she spoke a little about dying—*dying
is a process*, she said, *death is an endpoint. Or a threshold, if that's
what you believe.* When we are dying, she told us, one by one we
have to let go of those things that are precious to us, things we
thought we needed to make it through our days. And so she had
us cross three things off of our list, those things we would be
able to let go of first, because we couldn't move forward, toward
the end, with everything. I looked at my list. I felt like I'd been
tricked. I'd already distilled everything in my life down to these
ten things, and now I had to distill further. Muttering, I crossed
off Paris, I crossed off photography, I crossed off my truck. The
facilitator let us talk to the person next to us about what we had
let go of. Now I would have to bicycle everywhere, now I would
never make it back to Paris, now I would have to live with the
photographs I'd already taken. *Now,* the facilitator said, *cross*

off three more. Hater. I crossed off the ocean. I crossed off the shelter. I crossed off all my ex- and future lovers. I was down to four—my friends (I shifted my then-lover over to this list), my writing, my body, and the one photograph I had of me with my mother. I felt desperate. The facilitator said to cross off two more. Vengeful god, this posed a real problem. If I crossed off my body, could I still exist? Without friends who would catch me when I fell? Could I hold the image of my mother in my mind, without that photograph, when my memory was so bad? If I could no longer write, would anything ever make sense?

Ten years later I will begin writing the book about working with the homeless, but I will leave out the part where I killed a guy. "Kill" is a strong word, I know, I know—I didn't put my boot on John Doe's head and push him under the waves, but I also know that I wandered through the next many years feeling as if I had.

proteus (sciamachy)

Since we invaded Iraq, when I give a reading, I often read a poem by Saadi Youssef, simply to have an Iraqi voice in the room with us.

> America, we are the dead.
> Let your soldiers come.
> Whoever kills a man, let him resurrect him.
> We are the drowned ones, dear lady.
> We are the drowned.
> Let the water come.

Fanny Howe writes:

> *What I have been thinking about, lately, is bewilderment as a way of entering the day as much as the work. . . .*

> *There is a Muslim prayer that says, "Lord, increase my bewilderment," and this prayer belongs both to me and the strange Whoever who goes under the name of "I" in my poems—and under multiple names in my fiction—where error, errancy, and bewilderment are the main forces that signal a story. . . .*

Bewilderment breaks open the lock of dualism (it's this or that) *and peers out into space* (not this, not that).

Bewilderment as a way of entering the day. My terror with being a father, with having a child, if I can name it, is not the threat of some abstract maniac snatching her—it is that I will look at her and not feel a thing. That she will appear and nothing will change. That I won't be able to take her in, I won't be able to enter the day, not fully. That I might simply get in my car one day and drive, away from her, away from myself, that I won't remember. My fear has always been with myself, it has always been the fear of my own shadow. Maybe "Proteus" is simply another name for "shadow"—the shadow you drag behind you with every step, except when you walk in darkness, when you yourself become the shadow. The question, then, is not how Proteus knows what most terrifies you, but how it has come to pass that you don't recognize your own innermost fears—*Let the water come.*

four

istanbul

(2007) Inez and I are based in L.A. for a few months while she works on a new tv series (Inez is an actress). During the weeks of taping she starts to show, subtly at first, then undeniably. At one point the scriptwriters consider writing in that she has an eating disorder, but in the end they simply make her pregnant.

In August I fly from L.A. to New York, to connect with another airline, which will carry me to Paris, then on to Istanbul. Istanbul, I know, is far away—half in Europe, half in Asia—but still, I didn't expect it to take three days to get there, and it wouldn't have, if the jet from L.A. hadn't run out of gas on the way to New York. I'd never been on a jet that ran out of gas. It felt like when I was sixteen and would put fifty cents in my tank to make a run to the package store. We had to touch down in Rochester to refuel—"touch down," the pilot said, but seven hours later we were still stranded, and I had missed my connecting flight.

I'd been invited to Istanbul by a lawyer who is gathering testimonies from ex-detainees of Abu Ghraib. This lawyer is putting together a lawsuit against two American companies that have allegedly profited from torture—when I heard this I'd tracked her down. The lawsuit may or may not ever come to trial, which

is why she invited me, along with a handful of other artists—
she recognizes the need to get the information out through various alternative, nontraditional channels, not just through the
courts. Now, if asked, I'll sometimes say that I went to Istanbul
to bear witness, though at the time I was somewhat bewildered
as to my role. I sat at a table and took notes, and then I went
back to America and told people what I'd heard. By the time
I made it home, my daughter was two weeks closer to being
born.

istanbul (dream, reality)

By the time I land in Istanbul I'm so jetlagged, so bone-tired, that in the taxi to the hotel I'm almost hallucinating. We pass men in their underwear swimming in the Bosphorus, we pass fields of weekend picnickers sprawled out on ornate fabrics in the sun. Traffic sounds, a muezzin, a pop song on the radio—everything is calling us to prayer.

The taxi drops me off at the Armada Hotel. I check in and ask where the lawyers are, and within a few minutes I knock on the door to room 223. After brief introductions I find myself sitting next to a man telling the story of how he ended up in a photograph, a photograph I have seen many times by now, a photograph the whole world has seen. A photograph is like a house—once it is made we then start counting the days and then the years from when it was made. My eyes took a moment to adjust to the light. *Tell me what happened next*, the lawyer whispers.

~

I had a dream about this room before I found myself here. In the dream the room was the size of a barn, with six spaces divided by hastily built half-walls. In each room there was a shackle screwed into the floor, nothing more than a large eyebolt, really, and I worried that this eyebolt wasn't strong enough. It needed to be strong enough to hold a man. It needed to be like the shackles I had seen in the photographs, cemented into the floors. The rooms were dark, empty, the prisoners hadn't been brought in yet. I thought to leave a candle, and a lighter, but then I thought the man would use the lighter to set fire to his shackles, or to himself, or to the whole barn. In the dream I ended up leaving the candle and lighter in a corner, and if the man could reach them, if he knew to look, then come what may.

~

The room turns out to be utterly mundane—well lit, carpeted, a hotel room that one could find in any major city. The bed has been removed, and in its place is a table. The lawyer sits at the table, across from the ex-detainee. Another lawyer sits next to her, typing out the transcript of the conversation on a laptop. The translator sits at the head of the table, between the lawyer asking the questions and the ex-detainee. There is also an artist present, seated away from the table, near the window, painting a watercolor portrait in a large book, its pages folded like an accordion. When he isn't painting the portrait, he fills in the white space around the painted head with bits of what is being said. The seat next to the ex-detainee is empty, and this is where I sit, my notebook open.

transmogrification

When I was younger I worked for gangsters for a few years—
mostly they just smuggled drugs, though there was a story of
a kidnapping, and another story of a body found in the trunk
of a car. My mother dated one of them—he'd disappear a couple times a year, come back two months later, flush with cash.
After high school, when it was clear I was going nowhere, he
got me a job down at the pier, unloading fishing boats. In my
mind I was being groomed to make a run, to take a boat down
to Colombia, pilot it back full of marijuana, and likely this was
true. It was simple—I'd grown up broke, we were still broke,
and these gangsters, our friends, had found a way out.

~

Years later, when I move to New York, I will live in Brooklyn
with an artist—David—who will become one of my closest
friends. David grew up with money. Once we'd known each
other for a few years, I told him about my misspent youth,
about my plan of making a run, all of which he had a hard time
processing, especially the part about how I knew I'd put myself
in a position where I might have needed to carry a gun, which
meant I might have needed to use it. *No way,* he said, *you'd never*

do that. I tried to explain that it wasn't something I was proud of, it wasn't something I would have *wanted* to have done, but at that point, when I was eighteen, nineteen, I was willing to put myself in the position where it *might* happen.

What I was trying to say, maybe, is that I don't know what it is I'm capable of transforming into. When I was nineteen I knew the consequences of getting onto a boat laden with drugs, I knew the consequences of carrying a gun, and part of me was willing to do it anyway, or at least to consider doing it. Why? As a fictionalized John Lennon said, in a fictionalized version of his life, when asked how he'd managed to drive himself so hard, for so many years—*I was just fucken desperate.*

istanbul (the happy-bus)

It is likely you have seen the photograph of the naked man being dragged by a leash out of a cell by a girl named England— let's call him Amir. This is the third time the lawyers have met with Amir. The first time was in Amman, Jordan, where he told about his years in Abu Ghraib. The second time was six months ago, in Istanbul, when a team of doctors examined him, to corroborate his scars. This time is for him to look through the binders of the now-infamous photographs, to identify who and what he can. A painting on the wall behind his head depicts a scene from Turkey's past—peacocks and lions mingling together in a sultan's garden, a dark-skinned slave tending over it all.

Amir was a businessman awaiting a shipment of air conditioners from Iran when the CIA broke into his hotel room and arrested him. He was in his late twenties then. When we get to the photograph of him being dragged by the leash, he stops. *I remember that night*, he says, *I remember everything.* And then he tells us the story. The lawyer never takes her eyes off his face as he speaks, softly repeating, *And then what happened, and then what*, as he tells of his body being dragged from room to room, cell to cell.

It is only a year since Amir was released from prison. The

soldiers called the day of his release "the happy-bus day." *Tomorrow you will get to ride on the happy-bus*, they told him. Today, a year later, Amir shakes his head as he looks at the photographs of himself from that time—*I cannot recognize myself as that man*, he says. *Can you?*

two dogs

Two dogs live inside me, a woman in Texas tells me, *and the one I feed is the one that will grow.* She tells me this as a way to explain why she won't have coffee with me, ever—married, kids, happy, but sometimes her mind wanders, sometimes she thinks that another man, one that looks at her with kindness, one that seems to listen, is the answer, though she is unsure of the question. The thing is, her husband does all these things for her—he listens, he's kind, there's desire, everything's fine.

But still, still, these two hungry dogs.

Wait—this woman didn't say her dogs were hungry, did she? But aren't all dogs hungry? *Here Shadow, here Eros. Here Thanatos, here Light.* The one she feeds is the one that will grow, but does that mean that the other one will grow smaller? Will it grow so small as to vanish? Do the dogs that live inside her come from some Alice-in-Wonderland world? Are they fighting inside her, does she love them both, does she sometimes think if one died it would be easier? But then she'll have one dog inside her and the corpse of another dog—what good will that do, in the long run, what with all the other corpses we eventually end up dragging around inside us?

istanbul (the word made flesh)

There is a moment in Amir's story, as there will be in every story, when words are not enough, a moment when the only way to tell us what happened is to show us what they did to his body. At this moment he pushes back from the table and stands—*They hang me this way*, he says, and raises his arms out to his side as if crucified in the air. Something about him standing, about his body suddenly rising up, completely unhinges me, something about it makes his words real in a way they hadn't been before. At this moment I get it: these words are about his body, it was his body this story happened to, the body that is right here beside me, in this room I could barely even imagine just yesterday, his body that is now filling the air above our heads, our eyes upturned to see him. Amir stands there like that, arms outstretched—the scribe has nothing to write, the painter has nothing to paint, the interpreter has nothing to interpret, the lawyer's eyes are fixed on his eyes, all his words have led to this moment, when his body is finally allowed to speak. The lawyer shakes her head slightly. *And what happened next*, she says softly, and he lowers his arms and sits.

all living things have shoulders

(1996) For those few years when I worked in New York City public schools as an itinerant poet—Crown Heights, Harlem, the South Bronx—I'd lug a satchel heavy with books on the train every morning. Much of what I taught was directed toward finding out what the students saw every day. It was a way to honor their lives, which isn't generally taught in public schools. The beginning exercises were very simple: Tell me one thing you saw on the way into school this morning. Tell me one thing you saw last night when you got home. Describe something you see every day, describe something you saw only once and wondered about from then on. Tell me a dream, tell me a story someone told you, tell me something you've never told anyone else before. No one, in school at least, had ever asked them what their lives were like, no one had asked them to tell about their days. In this sense it felt like a radical act. I tried to imagine what might happen if each of them knew how important their lives were.

In the schools I'd visit, I'd sometimes pick up a discarded sheet of paper from the hallway floor, something a student had written in his notebook and then torn out. Sometimes, I could tell that he'd been given an assignment, and that he'd tried to fulfill it, and by tearing it out it was clear that he felt he had somehow failed. Out of all the ephemera I've bent down to collect from black and green elementary school linoleum floors over the years, one has stayed with me. Likely it was part of a research paper, likely for biology. It started with a general statement, which was, I imagine, meant to be followed by supporting facts. The sentence, neatly printed on the first line, was this: *All living things have shoulders*—after this there was nothing, not even a period, as if even as he was writing it he realized something was wrong, that he would never be able to support what he was only beginning to say, that no facts would ever justify it. All living things have shoulders—the first word is pure energy, the sweeping "All," followed by the heartbeat of "living"— who wouldn't be filled with hope having found this beginning? Then the drift begins, into uncertainty—"things"—a small misstep, not so grave that it couldn't be righted, but it won't be easy. Now something has to be said, some conclusion, I can almost hear the teacher, I can almost see what she has written on the blackboard—"Go from the general to the specific"—and what could be more general than "All living things," and what could be more specific than "shoulders"? He reads it over once and knows it can never be reconciled, and so it is banished from his notebook. *All living things have shoulders*—this one line, I have carried it with me since, I have tried to write a poem from it over and over, and failed, over and over. I have now come to believe that it already is a poem.

All living things have shoulders. Period. The end. A poem.

istanbul (the americans)

At times, in the silence between when a question is asked and when the translator translates it and when the answer is given, the only sound is the *clink clink clink* of the artist cleaning his brush in a glass of water. After four hours we finish going over the photographs with Amir, and we are all completely drained. As we stand to thank him, he reaches into his bag and takes out a camera. It looks so odd in his hands. He asks the translator to ask us to stand against one wall—he gestures toward it. We all move, awkwardly, to one corner of the room, gather together in front of a painting of a hammam. Amir raises the camera to his eye and smiles—*You see, it's not only the Americans who like to take photographs.*

immersion (hotel pool)

Swim, until the world becomes water, swim to the center of the pool, practice hanging, practice drowning, raise your arms above your head, let your body sink. Think of it as practice, for when they come—there is only so much they can do with your body. Swim to the ladder, hang from it as you catch your breath, let your arms hang behind you, like wings, then sink slowly into the water. Your arms will raise to shoulder height behind you, then to your ears—any further and they will dislocate. No one is forcing you to do this, you do it because you have heard that it is done to others. Sink further and you will sign the confession, you will give names, you will say whatever they tell you to say. But when they check your story it will be water, it will slip through their hands. On the confession you will have signed the name "Bird," because that's what you think, hanging there, your arms behind you. *All living things have shoulders*, you think, hanging there.

five

monkey-mind

Some Buddhists believe that as you wander the bardo, that realm between living and dying, you will encounter the physical manifestations of that which terrifies you. Over and over they will appear before you—this is your karmic debt, and only those who are enlightened will walk unafraid. Some believe that enlightenment often comes at the moment of death, just as it can often come at the moment of birth. Most of us, though, spend our given time—our handful of hours, our teaspoonful of years—hovering between these two poles, muddying the water. *Monkey-mind*, some call it. *Samsara*.

~

(2007) In Istanbul, while collecting testimonies, we asked each ex-detainee to describe the room where his torture took place. Each man looked around him—*It looked like this room*, each responded. *There was a table, there was a computer, someone was always behind me.* What did the person who tortured you look like, was the next question, and the detainee would look at me, then look at the artist, the only two white men in the room, and either point to him, or point to me—*He looked like him*, was the answer.

In some ways we were mere shadows to them.

One evening, over dinner in an outdoor restaurant, Amir asked if I was married, if I had children. I've been asked this question for years, whenever I travel, and I've been looked at with something like pity when I've answered no. *My first child will be born in January*, I told Amir. *A girl*. He narrowed his eyes and smiled, as if I had just come into focus.

twice

(1986) A fortune-teller (maybe she was a star-reader), the friend of a friend, laid some tarot cards out in a pattern on a piece of brocade. We were on Captain Jack's Wharf, in Provincetown, the water below us black as a mirror. She looked at the cards for a long while, then asked me when I'd been born, what time of day. I didn't know, I've never known, for some reason it's not on my birth certificate. The fortune-teller told me that she saw something in the cards about my mother, something I needed to know, and the time I was born would help her. It would mean something. The fortune-teller didn't know anything about my mother, as far as I knew. I thought it was hokum (*three p.m.? ten a.m.?*), but I also wondered what she might say, if I did know the time.

A few weeks later I dreamt that I was in the waiting room of a hospital, a woman I thought might be my mother in the far corner, looking away from me, looking out the window at the city. Distant, barely there. As one does in dreams, I went to her, touched her shoulder. She turned to face me—yes, it was her, I could have wept. I said, *I need to know what time I was born*, and she slowly answered, *You were born twice—once at five in the morning, and then again two days later.* Then she turned her face to the window and said no more.

the inventor of the life raft

Each Christmas my mother would have a boyfriend—sometimes a new one, sometimes one left over from the year before. This boyfriend would buy my brother and me a couple gifts, make Christmas, well, *Christmasy*. Each boyfriend, it seemed, was like a life raft—all you had to do was pull yourself up, or let your body be pulled up. But a life raft is, by definition, temporary. It could get you through the storm, but you couldn't live on it forever.

~

(2003) I was back from Rome for a few months, living in Provincetown again—*the last resort*, the locals call it. One of my favorite spots, perhaps on the planet, is Hatches Harbor, an inlet between two beaches where at high tide the ocean rushes in and fills the flats with seawater that then warms in the sun. You can shallow-dive the swollen pools or swim against the current or simply float in the sun half-submerged. You want to get there just as the tide turns, when the water is rushing back out and your body can be carried along by the current's invisible force. At the mouth of the inlet there is a riptide, an undertow, and it will carry you a few hundred feet out into the open bay if you don't know to swim hard across the current back to the shore.

———

Anna and I knew each other peripherally—we'd emailed a couple times to talk about poetry, and at some point she told me she'd be on the Cape for a few days, so we arranged to meet up. I even offered her a place to crash if she needed it. We spent our first day together hiking across the dunes at high tide, to swim in these tidal pools. On the way we talked about the relationships we were both in, about our doubts. She was about to move in with her boyfriend of six years, and part of her felt she was making an awful mistake. My girlfriend at the time—the playwright—had stayed in Rome for the summer. I told Anna my doubts about being able to meet this woman in eternity. Perhaps both of us knew these stories were merely versions of larger stories, meant to justify what we were doing at that moment (*take her hand, pull yourself up, or let your body be pulled up*). When we got to the water we dove in, our bodies carried effortlessly to the mouth of the inlet.

That night, back at the house, after dinner, we lingered until we had to say goodnight, and then we went to our separate rooms. But we left the door between us open, and continued to talk, from our beds, until the space between our words grew larger, and at some point in the silence one of us called out, *Are you sleeping?* The other answered, *I can't.* One asked, *Are you cold?* The other answered, *Yes*—and *yes* was the word that led me to her bed. I climbed the ladder to the loft, pulled aside the comforter, her body there, in my t-shirt, a glimpse of her underwear, her eyes, and as I put my body close to hers, the space between us filled with heat, and we lay like that, silent now, as minutes passed.

facts about water

1. Fish remember for only three seconds, then they forget.
2. On Antarctica you must move continually just to stay in one place.
3. Everything that swims in the ocean eventually sinks to the bottom and decays.
4. The ocean is always looking for a way into your boat.

These random facts, things you've taken in, for some reason are still rattling around in your brain. The purpose of the brain is to filter out 93 percent of what is taken in—this, again, is simply a fact.

Here's another fact:

The last words my mother wrote, perhaps the last thought she ever thought, were these—*Everyone knows each other so much longer.* If I've told you this already, forgive me (*samsara*)—before this is over it's likely I'll tell you again. What I didn't tell you (did I?) were her first words, the first sentence, of that same suicide note—*I don't know why I chose today to begin.*

I don't know why I chose today to begin.

First thought, best thought.

Strange verb, in this context, *to begin.*

First thought, last thought.

~

If I tell you that my mother had a problem with painkillers, that she worked nights as a bartender, that she dated a gang-ster, what goes through your head? If I say that the pills were for migraines, that she also worked at a bank, that she never missed a day of work, that I grew up feeling loved by her, that sometimes still I meet the old gangster for lunch when I'm in Boston, do these facts still fit your idea of her? If I say that it doesn't matter to me if you get a clear picture of her or not, that even if I could somehow bring her back, let you sit across from her, ask your questions, you would still have no idea who she was. I barely knew her, yet I knew her completely. When I was younger I would wait up for her to come home from work, I'd wait in her bed. I'd be asleep when she came in, she'd shut off the television, push me over to one side, and I'd wake up in the morning beside her. If it was Sunday I'd go into the kitchen and cook her some eggs, and if her feet hurt I'd rub them while she ate. Some weekends we went into Boston, to the cat show or the flower show, and other weekends we drove down to New-port, to wander the grounds of the mansions. Some weekends we went to her father's house—the big house—for lunch, and some mornings she stayed in bed with a migraine, and on those mornings I'd keep the television turned down low, offer to rub her temples. One afternoon we drove into Boston with my brother to see Monty Python's *Holy Grail* at the Beacon Theater, which was nearly empty except for us. As the lights dimmed, my mother began to laugh, from some silliness in the opening credits, and she never stopped, until her laughter got so loud that my brother and I moved away from her, up into the balcony, each of us laughing now in our separate corners of that old dark theater, our eyes filled with tears.

~.

I was reading *Paradise Lost* when my mother died, finishing my junior year at college, and for some days, maybe weeks, afterward, I roamed campus like a ghost. It felt like my body was trapped in a bubble, the walls of which were difficult to push beyond (*The Mind is its own Place, and there within, can make a Hell out of Heaven, or a Heaven out of Hell*). It felt somehow benign—inside that bubble everything became safe, because nothing really mattered. Some of this benign sensation was drug-induced—*self-medicating*, I called it. *Marijuana maintenance*. It made the world simple—some days I swear all I had to do was to think of someone for that person to appear before me. If I was lonely, which I was, every night, I could knock on a friend's door, I could just show up, and she, whoever she was, would take me in. Of course, there was a lot I couldn't do. Like fall asleep. Like wake up. Like feel anything. Like stop feeling everything. So every night I slept with someone, someone else, another friend. It was easy, putting my body into another's body—*We seem good at it*, I'd think, hovering a few feet above the bed. After my mother died, I still had a body, but it was not one I could enter, not one I could use. I was here, standing before you, only it was temporary—think of a snake, how it leaves its skin behind, and this skin looks like a snake at first, until you step on it and it powders. Then, after many disembodied years, a woman gave my body back to me. *Slow*, Inez said, *go slow. Don't come yet*, she said, *stay here with me.*

echo

One day you will hear yourself repeating something you once said to an old lover—*I'm not really in any shape to see anyone*, or, *No blame if it doesn't work out*. One day you will hear yourself saying these same words to a new lover—maybe you think it'll put her (him) at ease, as it seemed to put the other one at ease, and it might even be true. Or it might be that some part of you senses that it won't be forever, and you don't want to take responsibility for the heartache it (you) might bring. Or it might be simply your shadow talking, tricking you, once again, into believing that what you are saying is real.

(2003) After our first day together, after swimming in tidal pools, after our one night together, after ending up in the same bed, Anna went back to Brooklyn. She moved in with her boyfriend, while I stayed on in that small seaside town. We'd talk on the phone when we could, but I tried to give her (me) space to figure out what I (she) needed. Near the end of summer she came once more to visit. Then she went back to Brooklyn, and her boyfriend read her journals, found out we'd slept together, and they broke up. In the weeks that followed, I'd look forward to when we'd speak, to when we'd see each other next. I'd go to

her whenever I made it to Brooklyn, show up at her door after midnight. She'd answer it in her bathrobe, take me in.

That fall I closed on the rundown Victorian upstate, just in time to celebrate the anniversary of my mother's death and to end the relationship with the playwright. I sat in my newfound ruin, on the orange shag carpet, the cheap paneling on the walls, wondering what I'd done, unsure if I'd made a terrible mistake. Anna invited me to go Mexico with her for Christmas, but I told her, told myself, that I needed time to be on my own. A week or so later I invited all my friends up, and twenty of us slept over, on couches and air mattresses. I set up a Christmas tree in that unfinished house, made a big dinner, and later we all had a snowball fight. The worst was behind us, I told myself.

In January, I fly to Texas, to begin my first semester of teaching. Anna and I talk on the phone every couple days, remember what we'd read, what we'd seen, and at some point I'd ask if she was touching herself and she'd say she was. *Whatever you want me to do I will do,* I'd say.

In May, when the semester ends, I make my way back north, back to the house. With the windows open, the shag carpet ripped up, the paneling torn off the walls, it isn't so tomblike. The backyard is thick with tiger lilies. I feel more hopeful. It's May—everywhere in the world looks good in May. For the first time I can imagine spending some time there, in that part of the world, in that house. It could be beautiful, this life. I make my way to Brooklyn once a week or so, to see Anna. I'm still in no shape to see anyone, not fully, and this still seems to be okay with her. Back upstate I hire a friend, a carpenter—Philip— to help me transform the house. As will happen when a project stretches out from weeks to months, Philip and I hang out more and more. One night, at his house for dinner, I meet Inez. Unbeknown to either of us, Philip's partner, Caroline, had seen something in me when we met, and thought of Inez. The dinner that night was a set-up.

the tricky part

(2004) I call Inez two days after I meet her. I invite her to a play in New York that a friend had written and was starring in, a one-man show called *The Tricky Part*. Later that night, back at her place, we talk about whether or not we ever thought about having children. I say what I always say—I've always imagined that, one day, I'd have a child, that I'd be a father, but it's hard to see when, or to imagine what that day will look like. We kiss a little, but I tell her my love life is a little complicated at that moment, that it is maybe not the best time to jump into something. We kissed a little more. We weren't asking each other if we could imagine having children with each other, but we weren't not asking that either.

For years I'd told myself that I could live anywhere, for a year or two. I told myself I could be happy (or unhappy) anywhere. When I'd go to a new city, I'd try to imagine myself living there, and I always could. Some part of me did this with women as well, some part of me imagined a new woman as a city I could stay in for a while, then visit from time to time. I'd know my way around, I wouldn't need a map, but I wouldn't really live there either. But a child? A child wasn't like a city, or even a woman. I couldn't simply visit now and then.

mistress yin

(2006) A friend is in town for a few days from San Francisco. I ask him if he wants to go with me to a play, a retelling of *Ulysses* called *Dead City*. It's in a theater called 3-Legged Dog, down near the hole that was the World Trade Center. We meet up beside ground zero, then wander for a while, killing time before the show, catching up. As we turn a corner onto another ordinary-looking street, he stops, excited. *Wait*, he says, pointing down the block—*I've been in this neighborhood before. Mistress Yin's is right there—she's got the best dungeon in town.*

A few days later I attend an event he's organized, a reading in midtown to raise money to support Democratic candidates in the upcoming elections, focusing on close races in Ohio, Pennsylvania, Arizona. As I walk in, my friend is talking to a woman near the bar, and he introduces her to me as Yin. As she takes my hand, my friend remembers—*Yin's the one I was telling you about*, he shouts over the din, *the one with the dungeon.*

Nice to meet you, I say, still holding her hand. Clear-eyed, modestly dressed, beautiful—remarkably ordinary-looking, I think, though what did I expect? *I'd like to see your dungeon sometime*, I tell her, unsure what I mean by it.

Sure, she says, looking directly at me—*you can come by anytime.*

A few minutes later I overhear Yin say the word "torture."

I'm writing about torture, I say, jumping in, interrupting.

Not that kind of torture, Yin says, and turns away.

story of o

In *Story of O*, the sadomasochistic French novel, the O of the title is an abbreviation of the narrator's name (Odile), but the O has also been read to mean nothing, zero, emptiness. A cipher, a hole, a cunt. O is the first letter of the word "object," thereby, some argue, signifying a woman objectified. I bought it twenty-five years ago, right after my mother died, and then it took twelve years to finally open it, and now it sits unopened, once again, on my desk. Shortly after I first read it, thirteen years ago now, the identity of the author was revealed, and if I remember correctly she was the lover, the mistress, of a married man, high up in the literary world. She wrote the book as a way to seduce him, to hold him, when it seemed he was going to give up on the affair, and, the story goes, it worked. In *Story of O* a woman obliterates herself, or allows herself to be obliterated, for the love of a man.

~

Here's something I try not to think about much:

In the body of her suicide note, on the second or third page, my mother described herself as "a real *Story of O*." This, still, is not something I have found a way to understand, not fully. My mother, as I've mentioned, had several boyfriends when I was growing up—I met most of them, liked many, but her sexual life, her *predilections*, were not on display. As far as S&M goes, there was no evidence in what I saw of her relationships, but much of the business of relationships, obviously, takes place in the shadows. I only have this one reference to a book in the last thing she would ever write—a glimmer that pulls on my (sub)consciousness still, but a glimmer of what?

~

Story of O opens with O being driven by her lover to a chalet in the countryside on the outskirts of Paris, and once there she is subjected to torture and rape, to which she eventually submits. I reread the beginning of it just now, and was surprised that it wasn't more consensual, as I'd remembered it. O, from the outset, is coerced, and yes, she submits, but under threat. The book is, as a whole, charged, erotic, and incredibly depressing. When I read it the first time, it struck me as both a parable and a critique of Catholicism. O takes certain Catholic concepts— mortification of the flesh, the crucifixion as love—to their logical conclusions. O is in love, and her lover asks her to sacrifice, until by the end of the book she is being led around a party on a leash, naked but for a feathered mask.

~

Here's something else I try not to think about much:
    While making love, sometimes, Anna wanted me to get a little rough, but I couldn't, not really, not what she wanted, not

for long. One night she put my hands to her throat, wrapped her hands over mine, squeezing my fingers tighter until it—I—made her gag. Erotic asphyxiation, California dreaming, suffocation roulette, I knew what it was, but it confused me, or maybe what I felt was closer to terror (*Proteus, listen, this is what terrifies me—how did I, how will you, turn into this?*). I pulled my hands away, kissed her eyes, murmured, *Your body's so precious, so precious*, a contrite Gollum. We never talked about it, and now I wish we had—I wanted us to be enough, without hurting each other any more than we already were, than we soon would.

~

On the last few pages of *Story of O*, maybe the last page, O asks her lover to kill her, or to let her kill herself—I forget if he, or she, does, or doesn't. I seem to remember an alternative ending, but I cannot recall if both are in the text or not, nor can I remember which one I read. And I am not ready, not just yet, to open it again, not ready to enter into it again, not fully.

I don't know why I chose today to begin.

I open the book. I put it down.

proteus (dissolve)

(2004) This is the first year everyone tells me that I look different, that I look my age. *You used to be a pup*, one woman says—*now you're a dog*. I've made it past the age my mother was, the last year she reached, which was the same age my father was when he entered his first bank and robbed it. I think these things, but I don't say them. But even thinking them suggests that I imagine life as simply a roomful of boxes—a box marked glass, a box marked papers, a year magic-markered on each. Boxes of tax receipts, boxes of old love letters, one year has to be the last year, and then the next year there will be no box, no year scrawled on the side.

~

The last thing I'll say about my mother's suicide note (even I don't believe this is the last thing I'll say) is that she wrote it twice—what I mean is that she began it once and then either reconsidered or else whatever she took didn't shut out all the lights, so two weeks later she picked up the pen again, after she'd taken some more pills and walked down to Peggotty Beach, but once there found herself unable to throw her body into the ocean. I know all this because this is what she wrote in her letter. Back home she picked up the pen again, maybe she took some more pills, because the longer she wrote the more her handwriting began to break up, as the pills began to dissolve, to seep into every pore, making her words, by the last page, hard to decipher. She stood at the edge of the ocean, then she found her way back home, she must have found her way back, because that's where my brother found her.

six

the falling is the rain

(2007) The due date is an approximation, an estimate—*She can come any day now*, the doctor tells us. Manifest already, her hand waving against the tight skin of Inez's belly, but to me, somehow, it is all still deeply abstract. One day, soon (we hope), she will make her way into this world, she will open her eyes and breathe and cry, but beyond that I don't know a thing. What I mean is, I have no idea what will happen within me at that moment. Will she suddenly become real to me? Will something heretofore unknown bloom inside my body? Right now it feels like I'm on the slow ascent of a rollercoaster, the car climbing the rickety hill, just before the fall. And so, for now, when I'm not reading transcripts from Abu Ghraib—from the soldiers who were following orders, to the man on the end of the leash, to the private contractors who wish it could all be more professional—I'm reading what I can about children. *It is joy to be hidden, but disaster not to be found*, Winnicott reminds me.

~

The week after I get back from Istanbul, I go on a meditation retreat with Thich Nhat Hanh, the Vietnamese monk and teacher. I've been studying with him off and on (mostly off) for eighteen years now. The plan is to sit for a week in silence, to listen as he speaks, but I end up talking more than I'd expected. My dharma discussion group's focus is addiction, and a handful of us addicts climb a great maple tree each afternoon to talk among the branches until sunset.

Thich Nhat Hanh says it is a mistake to say "the rain is falling," to say "the wind is blowing." *What is rain if it is not falling? What is wind if it is not blowing? The falling* is *the rain, the blowing* is *the wind*.

The next day, in the tree, I bring it up.

He's talking about impermanence, someone says.

It's the same reason we climb trees, someone else offers—*to remind us that we were all once monkeys.*

lightning, pond

(2004) When we first got together, I told Anna that I'd likely see other people, and when Inez and I first got together, I told her about Anna. I'm being upfront, I tell myself. A few months into seeing Inez, over the phone, in a lurching, imperfect attempt to maintain clarity, I tell Anna that I am on my way to the train station to pick up a friend (Inez) who'll be staying with me for the weekend. Anna asks if she's a lover. *Yes,* I tell her. Anna is silent for a long time. I ask if she's alright, and she answers, *I'm afraid I might hurt myself.* I don't think about her words much at the time, not consciously, not because I take them lightly, but because they sink in so deeply. It's the way I walk through the world, carrying that fear, that the beloved will go, will die, and that I will be the one to blame. Maybe her words did to me what they sometimes do, maybe they flipped the switch inside me, the switch that starts the tape, the tape that murmurs over and over, *You can save her,* over and over, *This time you won't fail.* Or maybe her words flipped the other switch, the one that starts the other tape, the one that murmurs, *Go ahead.* The one that hisses, *I'm not going to miss you if you do.*

~

One night that August I have a dream: I'm in a crowded court-room, on trial. Someone is being sentenced before I am to be sentenced—I can't remember if his sentence was light or if it was death. Next it is my turn. The judge asks if I should be under house arrest, or if I should go to prison for two days. I say that I should go to prison, and the courtroom erupts into sustained applause—I have said the right thing, everyone knows that I deserve to go to jail. A friend is being sentenced after me, and he chooses to go to prison as well, because I have. The dream ends with me fearing I have made a mistake, fearing the violence that awaits us.

~

As summer slips into fall I spend a week in Provincetown. As the ocean gets too cold, I drive myself to the pond every day. One day, undressing at the shore, the sky dark and getting darker, I hear a distant rumble. I step into the water, and it gets louder. I was hoping for the calm a swim usually brings, hoping to quiet the noise in my head, but instead I find myself imagining the storm, imagining lightning, imagining a bolt striking the water. I imagine racing it to the other side, and what will happen if I don't make it. I wonder how close it will have to strike for me to feel it, but I know that if it strikes the pond anywhere it will find me. Imagining lightning striking a pond as you swim across it is not like buying a gun, or even imagining buying a gun, but how does one measure how far it is from buying a gun? I swam all the way to the other side.

I show up at Anna's door a few more times that fall, even after my lurching attempt at honesty. *Why are you here?* she'd ask, and then she'd take my body into her hands. Much of what transpired in the following year took place in different cities, the two of us alone in this apartment or that, alone in strangely familiar hotel rooms, together or if not then talking on the phone after midnight. If the tape was still running in my head, I could no longer hear it. *Whatever you want me to do I will do.*

the invisible city

The first book I called mine, the first book I remember, was a picture book, *The Magic Monkey*—an old Chinese legend adapted by a thirteen-year-old prodigy, Plato Chan, and his sister, Christina. The monkey in the story, as I remember it, was a misfit—lost, wandering, aimless, trying to find his way home. He finagles his way into a walled school and there finds that he has magical powers, powers of transformation—he can change into a tree, a bird, a waterfall—but each thing he transforms into has a price, a complication. The tree becomes rooted, the waterfall slips away, the bird must constantly fly. I'm making this all up now from memory. I have the book on my bookshelf but I'm afraid to open it, in case I find out that the power it held over me proves to be thin, silly, superficial.

~

(2002) In Rome, month upon month, I struggled with how to structure the book about my father (*He already had the water, he just had to discover jars*). At one point I laid each chapter out on the terrazzo floor, eighty-three in all, arranged them like the map of an imaginary city. Some of the piles of paper, I imagined, were freestanding buildings, some were clustered into

neighborhoods, and some were open space. On the outskirts, of course, were the tenements—abandoned, ramshackled. The spaces between the piles were the roads, the alleyways, the footpaths, the rivers. The bridges to other neighborhoods, the bridges out. I'd walk along them, naming each building (tower of man-pretending-not-to-be-homeless), each neighborhood (the heights, the lowlands, the valley of lost names), each passageway (path of those-claiming-happy-childhoods). In this way I could get a sense if one could find their way through the book, if the map I was creating made sense, if it was a place one would want to spend some time in. If one could wander there, if one could get lost.

One morning, shortly after landing in Rome, I woke up ill— it felt like the flu. I needed to go out for juice and Tylenol, then I needed to get back into bed. I shuffled through the streets of the paper city, stepped out into the actual hallway, the door clicked shut behind me—at the sound of the click I knew I'd left my key inside. I had my cellphone, but it was still early, and the landlord, who'd become a friend, would not be awake for hours. I got some juice at the café, left some messages, and ended up sleeping on a bench in Piazza Vittorio. The city I'd been building, the book about my homeless father, was locked in the apartment I'd lost the key to. I woke to a group of schoolchildren marching past me. One asks his teacher, *Perche quell'uomo dorme fuori?*

unknown, known

(2005) When I bought the house upstate, a friend said it would change my life. *You will own a piece of the earth*, he said. *You will feel rooted.* But it didn't work out that way, not for me. Yes, I could appreciate the way the clematis strangled the maple, the way the doorknobs were all mismatched, but my natural-born restlessness only seemed to grow the more days I spent there. Rooted? I ended up staying in the house only to work on it, and then I'd leave. The idea that I owned a piece of the earth meant nothing. I knew that if one day I walked out the door and never came back I'd barely even remember it. I moved around more those first two years of owning a house than I ever had—I was vapor, I was air, I was nowhere.

Inez slept over one night, one of the few nights I slept in the house, and in the morning she drove to the local convenience store to get some cream for her coffee. Before she left she stood in the dining room, asked if I needed anything, said she'd be back in a minute. When I looked up a minute later she was still standing there, only it wasn't her—it was Anna. At dawn she'd driven up from Brooklyn, and let herself in when she saw Inez go out.

Tears in our eyes, she asked if I was in love with her.

I'm in love with both of you, I told her.

~

One day you will need to come up with a story about an old lover, as a way to understand, to explain, why it didn't work out. The one you woke up beside, dreaming of someone else. The one who wouldn't take you in her mouth. The one who wanted you to promise to meet her in eternity. The one who was angry with you every other day. The one destroying herself slowly. The one with two other boyfriends. The one who left a Polaroid of another man on the bedside table for you to find, standing there naked, his erection in his hand. And then there will be the more bewildering stories, the stories of lovers that should have worked out but didn't: The one you swore you'd swim to the bottom of the ocean to find and kiss back to life. The one who still fills every cell when you hear Macy Gray sing "I Try." The one you felt known with, finally known.

Whatever else I might say about my time with Anna, when I was with her I felt known, perhaps for the first time. *Known?* What that meant to me, if I had to define it, was that when we were together it seemed I could drag some part of my shadow into the light, especially the part that was uncertain about the next breath. Those rooms we shared became a space in which to reveal a darkness I carried inside me, a heaviness that needed to be dragged into the light, or it would sink me. Trouble was— maybe—that we shared the same dark impulses (*here eros, here thanatos*). In the end, maybe, our knowing lacked perspective, so, in the end we risked merely sinking each other. *God's loneliness and desire to be known set creation going.* Known—it was only later I realized it was the same word my father had used in his first letter to me, the same word my mother had used in her last letter to anyone. *Everyone knows each other so much longer*—these were her last words, the last words her hands would touch, the last few stones dropped into her deep, deep well. *The violence of God's sense of isolation sent the heavens into a spasm of procreating words that then became matter.* Then she put down her pen, then she picked up her gun—*here, bullet*—words that then became matter, the violence of God's sense of isolation.

seven

lava

A friend tells this, perhaps apocryphal, story: while living in Hawaii, a volcano erupted, and after the initial blast, which destroyed the top of the mountain and everything else in the vicinity, the lava continued to ooze slowly out, over the next several months, so slowly that you could walk up to the wall of it, put your hand on it, feel its warmth. How high was it? Twenty feet, I imagine, more or less. So high you'd have to tilt your head back to see the sky. The town my friend was staying in was downhill, spared the initial blast, but the lava kept coming. Then the scientists came, to calculate its movement, to predict how long it would take to reach the village, to mark which house would be the first to be swallowed beneath the slow-motion wave. Some argued that it was better than a flood, better than a fire—lava gives you time to move out what you most value, time to move everything, if you are able. If you are able you could move the entire house, but I had the idea that the island was small, the village against the sea, the only option would be to uproot your house and put it on a raft and float it to the next island. I had the idea that most simply went each day to the wall of lava, put their hands to it, hoped it would slow down, hoped it would run out of juice, hoped it would simply stop.

sheepfucker

(2003) The outcome of the current crisis is already determined—
our president assures us of this, a few months before we invade
Iraq. His certainty, it seems, is one of the traits his admirers are
drawn to. Through the first few months of the war this phrase
becomes my (cynical) mantra—*the outcome of the current crisis
is already determined*—I hate carrying it around, muttering it to
myself. I hate my self-satisfaction when each act of violence and
chaos in Baghdad seems to prove the president and his certainty
wrong. Until I begin to wonder if, just maybe, violence and
chaos are precisely the outcome he intended.

~

(2005) Sam Harris and I have an email correspondence for a
year or so after the photograph was taken of us shaking hands
and smiling, after I'd read his book which advocates the use of
torture. At one point I ask if he knows the sheepfucker joke:

> *A man, walking with a stranger through his village, points to
> the church—See that church, he says,* I built those walls
> with my own hands, dug the stones from my own fields.

The stranger looks up at the church, admires the craftsman-ship. But do you think anyone calls me William the Church Builder? *They walk a little farther, stop before the school. William points to it*—I raised the funds to have a new roof put on that school, *he tells the stranger,* worked for weeks without pay, but do you think anyone calls me William the Savior of our School? *William shakes his head.* But you fuck one sheep . . .

I point out to Harris that there is much to admire in *The End of Faith*, but, like the poor sheepfucker, when he advocates one little torture . . . Harris's certainty about the efficacy of torture to gather actionable intelligence surprises me, as it seems based on a blind faith, and his book is, ostensibly, against faith. The South African artist William Kentridge speaks to this type of certainty:

> *To say that one needs art, or politics, that incorporate ambigu-ity and contradiction is not to say that one then stops recog-nizing and condemning things as evil. However, it might stop one being so utterly convinced of the certainty of one's own so-lutions. There needs to be a strong understanding of fallibil-ity and how the very act of certainty or authoritativeness can bring disasters.*

The outcome of the current crisis is already determined.

the ticking is the bomb

Let's say you're a soldier in Iraq, assigned to a military prison. You are now Military Police, an MP, though you have not been trained for this. You've been told to soften up the prisoners before you, to get them ready to be interrogated the next day. Military Intelligence tells you this, though sometimes you are told it by CIA spooks, and sometimes by civilian contractors, whose names you don't know and who answer to no one. *Give them a bad night*, you've been told, so you give them a bad night—you strip them naked, you throw cold water on them, you do not let them sleep. The rules have changed, you've been told, the gloves have come off. One guy, whenever you knee him in the thigh, he cries *Allah*—it becomes a game to see how many times you can make him cry *Allah*.

Or let's say you've been trained as an interrogator. You've been told that one of the thousands before you has the answer that will save an American city from an attack. It might be the city your wife and child live in, you don't know, you will never know. You walk into a room, a man is hanging from the ceiling by his wrists, his arms pulled behind his back, a sack over his head. You've been told that the bomb is ticking, and in this room you swear you can almost hear it. You remove the sack, you take hold of this man's neck, you look into his eyes.

In order to continue to hold on, through your doubts and fears, you need to be certain of the outcome. You must push aside any bewilderment you have, ignore any questions besides the one question. *The outcome of the current crisis is already determined*—this is the kind of certainty you need to continue to hold on to the prisoner before you.

~

Imagine this:

You don't even have a child, not yet, but as a "thought experiment" you are asked what you will do when she is kidnapped, specifically what you will do with her kidnapper, who you have somehow captured, who now sits before you, in a windowless room, tied to a chair, refusing to tell you where she is hidden, refusing to answer your question. The clock is ticking, they say—*tick tick tick*—can you hear it?

The falling is the rain, the blowing is the wind.

So here I am—the maniac tied to the chair before me, let's call him Proteus. I've been told that a bomb is about to go off, potentially killing hundreds, or even thousands, of innocent people. As I hold on, as I ask him my question, as I listen for his answer, he transforms—into a dog on a leash, into a man dancing with panties on his head, into a bruise, into a madman, into a waterfall, into a cockroach in a bowl of rice. Into a man strapped into a chair, into thirty men strapped into thirty chairs, refusing to eat, thirty tubes forced down their noses.

So here I am, my fingers tight around Proteus's neck, asking my same question, over and over, as if the answer exists, inside the maniac, inside the prisoner, inside the beloved, inside my mother, inside my father, inside me, as if the answer is there and just needs to be released.

And here I am, holding my own head, dunking it into a bathtub full of water, repeating my meaningless question over and over, knowing that I will never get the question right.

And here I am, holding my breath, and then letting it go.

the fallen tower

(2006) In Assisi, in the lower basilica, is a series of Giotto frescoes—one depicts a fallen tower. Above this fallen tower another fresco depicts the Slaughter of the Innocents, and beside this a man speaks to a skeleton, and the skeleton appears to listen. In another panel a man dives headfirst from another tower—or perhaps it's the same tower that eventually falls— and no one seems to notice but one man, in the foreground, who raises a hand to catch him, though they are far apart.

The fallen tower is five stories tall, but now only one side remains standing. What we see is the ruined side—it looks like a bomb smashed into it, but in Giotto's time there were no bombs, were there? What could have brought it down? An earthquake? A catapult? The idea of a bomb? A third of the roof is intact, covering a third of the broken floor below it. On either side the bricks crumble, the wooden joists are cracked, the land- scape strewn with a muddle of debris. A child is being carried from the wreckage. Sixteen mourners stand in the foreground, rubble at their feet. The first, on the left, closest to the ruin, looks on, his hands stroking his chin, as if he is trying to under- stand something important. A few look to the ground, as if the answer is there. Only one looks away. Most are focused on the child's body—ashen with dust or death—on its back, held waist-high, the arm flung or merely hanging to the side. This is how one carries a sleeping child, I think. A woman kisses his face, another woman bends toward him, her hands clasped in prayer, while another woman keens, her face turned toward the sky. Two men on either side hold her hair away from her eyes. These three women touch their own faces, as if to feel the breath coming out of their mouths.

I am in Assisi to teach a poetry workshop, though to call what I do "teaching" always seems somewhat inaccurate. It feels more like simply standing at the bow of a ship as it makes its way through the fog. Our group meets in the morning, and every afternoon I take the bus up the mountain to an outdoor public pool, to swim for an hour surrounded by young Italians and cypress trees. At night I wander the medieval city, past groups of pilgrims holding hands and singing "kumbaya." One night in the lobby of the hotel we all watch *The Battle of Algiers*, the 1966 film about the disaster of the French occupation of Algeria. I'd never seen it, though it's been in the news lately—the Pentagon recently screened it to its generals in order to understand why things were going so wrong in Iraq.

At the pool one afternoon I see a boy wearing an orange shirt, these words stenciled on the back:

GUANTANAMO

CAMP X-RAY

A CELL IN HELL

527-0985-339

Had torture really transformed, so quickly—and while hundreds were still locked up, indefinitely—into the stuff of knock-off fashion?

the battle of algiers

The Battle of Algiers begins with a man in a room surrounded by soldiers. The man is in a chair, his back is to the camera. A man in a suit enters the room. *We got him talking*, one soldier tells the man in the suit. In the next scene a man in a white djellaba sits on a curb in a whitewashed city, his cart parked on the street beside him. An engine is strapped to the cart, the cart is on wheels. It is the size of a cart a hot dog vendor would push through the streets of New York, but this is not New York. We don't know what kind of machine this is, its purpose—maybe to heat tar, maybe to collect trash. All that is clear is that the man is weary, that he has pushed his cart to this spot, that he is resting.

After a few peaceful moments in the shade a white man in a white suit appears on a balcony above him, coming out into the sun tentatively, as if he has been hiding in the shadows, his eyes adjusting. He looks into the sky, as if to see if something is falling. He then looks down at the street, sees the Arab, points—*There*. Someone else emerges from the shadows, looks down, points. More come out onto their balconies, someone yells for the police to arrest him. The Arab is unaware for a while that he is the one they are yelling about—he doesn't understand their words. Then he hears sirens. He looks up, sees it is him they are pointing at. He then stands and walks quickly away, leaving his machine. A police car appears at the end of the street, blocking his way. The Arab turns, another police car appears beside him, he cannot walk further. In the next scene, in the interrogation room, we see his name written on a form, we see his address, we hear him say that he has a wife and three children.

That night one of the interrogators is at a lavish outdoor party. When he leaves he is driven through the shuttered city, the car moving freely through the curfew-quiet streets. The car pulls up to a building, we see it is the same street number the Arab gave them. The interrogator takes a box from the trunk, carries it into the courtyard, leaves it at a door. The box has a fuse, he lights it and walks back to the car and gets in and as he drives away the bomb explodes and the building falls.

For an hour or so after this explosion the film reenacts the ensuing chaos, a predictable cycle of retaliation and repression, until a general faces a group of reporters. *So let's talk about torture*, he says. *What if the prisoner remains silent for twenty-four hours. Legality can be inconvenient. We're neither madmen nor sadists. We are soldiers. Our duty is to win. If France is to stay in Algeria—if you say yes, then you must accept the consequences.* The consequences, as we know, is that France could not win, even though they tortured thousands of Algerians, or perhaps precisely because they did.

The morning after watching *The Battle of Algiers*, I'm in my room, preparing for our workshop. Assisi is a hill town, the Umbrian valley spread out below. The television is tuned to CNN, and live from Lebanon I see the same scene I'd just seen the night before—a building reduced to rubble, a child carried from the wreckage, a woman crying. My friend Tarek was emailing me from Beirut with updates, and to let me know that he was okay. Later that day I went to the Basilica, and saw Giotto's fallen tower, and stood before it for a long time.

istanbul redux

(2007) First the businessman, then the taxi driver, then the cleric (the translator calls him a "preacher"), then the ex-soldier, then the dentist—could they be any more ordinary? We collect their testimonies, the week goes on and on. Now it's a thirty-year-old student, telling of being picked up in a sweep, part of the recent "surge." U.S. soldiers kicked their way into his apartment in the middle of the night, while he slept with his pregnant wife. The soldiers pulled the both of them from bed, shone a light in their faces, asked him a question about a neighbor, a neighbor he didn't know, a question he could not answer. They threatened to take his wife into the next room, alone—*You know what that will mean*, they told him, but still he had no answer. He was then beaten and shackled and hooded and dragged from the house, thrown into a humvee, driven to a landing strip, thrown into a helicopter, until he eventually arrived at a building he now believes is near the airport, either in Mosul or Baghdad. Once inside this building, he found himself in a large room, maybe the size of a gymnasium, filled with black boxes lined up in rows. Maybe a hundred boxes, maybe two hundred, hard for him to say—he was hooded nearly constantly and quickly lost track of night and day. The boxes are about two and a half feet wide, five feet long. He was thrown into one of these boxes,

for days, which turn into weeks, unable to straighten his body, barely able to breathe. Every twenty or thirty minutes a soldier kicked the box, or hit it hard with a club, and it made his shackled body jump. Around him he could hear the screams and pleadings of his fellow prisoners—those with stomach pains, those with infections, those slowly going mad. Three years since the release of the photographs, and you can be assured that there will be no photographs of these boxes slipping out. What was once the vaguely directed actions of a bunch of amateurs on the night shift (if, in fact, that is what it was) has become professional, organized, sanctioned. Someone designed this room, someone fabricated these boxes, a memo went out telling the soldiers how often to bang on the side of the boxes, a memo we will likely never see. Among themselves the Iraqis call these boxes *tawabeet sood*, or *nash sood*—black coffins—I can't help thinking of them as the shadows of the flag-draped coffins we were also not allowed—or couldn't—or refused—to see.

eight

the broken bowl

In *The Child's Conception of Time,* Piaget claims that at some point in his or her development a child cannot tell which comes first—the photograph of a cup on a table, or the photograph of the same cup broken on the floor. Until the age of four it is just as likely the broken cup comes before the whole cup, that the floor is just another table, that milk can be poured into the broken cup, that the broken cup can be put back on the table and it will be whole again. I tell myself to try to remember this, for the day my as-yet-unborn daughter pours her milk into her broken bowl.

ravaged

On the first page of Duras's *The Lover*, a woman runs into a man on a Paris street, an ex-lover, someone she hasn't seen for years. *Everyone says how beautiful you were then*, he tells her, *but I prefer your face as it is now—ravaged*. I was twenty-two when I read it, and it made me want an ex-lover to find me when I was old, to tell me that she preferred me as I was, standing before her, ravaged.

I found Duras's *The Sea Wall* in a used bookstore a few years later, when I was living in Paris. As I remember it, a girl is living with her mother in a rundown estate in Indochina, the girl much like the girl in *The Lover*, who I took to be a version of Duras herself. The father is gone, missing, the money running out. And the sea, the China Sea, for some reason the sea is rising. Monsoons, maybe—yes, it's monsoon season, every year the sea rises, which is why a wall is needed. Only the wall is in disrepair and the father is missing and there isn't enough money to repair it. That's how I remember the story, though it could be all wrong. Let's just say it's how I want, or need, to remember it.

paradise lost

(2007) *Our thoughts create reality*—I pass this koan spray-painted on a Brooklyn sidewalk on the way to a friend's apartment. Later, in her studio, I saw a print of *Saint Michael and the Dragon*, painted by Crivelli in the fifteenth century. In Christian and pre-Christian iconography many saints are depicted slaying dragons, you've likely seen versions of this—a young man on horseback, or sometimes on foot, a dragon beneath his boot, his lance just piercing the dragon's flesh, or its point pushing into the beast's open mouth. In *Paradise Lost*, Milton wrote about Michael, the archangel who does battle with Satan in the Garden of Eden, just before he escorts Adam and Eve out. For years now, for some unknown reason, this dragon has found me, or maybe I'm simply drawn to him. One reason, perhaps, is that this dragon, this Satan, though subdued, is always still alive. He comes from that edge of perception where our shadow selves are almost tangible—we can never really kill this dragon, this shadow, because with it we will kill a part of ourselves. The trick is how to live with it without it consuming us, without allowing it to rise up so much that it takes charge. Underfoot, subdued, it keeps us in balance, it reminds us of the darkness we come from, of the darkness we are made of—if we don't acknowledge it, if we don't find a way to integrate it into our days, this darkness can manifest itself inside us as fear, then our fear can transform into rage, and we can find ourselves lashing out at shadows. Crivelli's Michael is reaching behind his back for his sword, and Satan's clawed hands are reaching up Michael's legs, almost caressing him. Michael and this devil stare into each other's eyes, as if they are each looking into a mirror, one illuminated, one in shadow.

mexico (the war)

I have a packet of photographs from when my grandparents were first married, before they had children, or maybe they'd simply left the kids at home. The photographs are of a roadtrip to Mexico, clearly from a time before everything fell apart. In each of the photographs they are smiling—maybe it was after my grandfather got back from the war, or else it was just before he shipped out. It could have been in the thirties. They had money during the Depression, they could have afforded a road-trip. These few photographs reveal more about their early life together than anything either one of them ever told me. In one blurry photograph my grandfather is flat on his back on a hotel bed, a bottle of what I imagine to be tequila rising straight up from his mouth to the ceiling, as if a flower is growing from his face, as if he is going to finally fill himself completely. I imagine my grandmother took this photograph, and I imagine her laughing gleefully as she did, having just taken a pull herself.

~

(2006) At one point, in the process of saying goodbye, or attempting to, once again, Anna and I spent a day together in my house in upstate New York. She saw a copy of Duras's memoir *The War* on my shelf. I'd only glanced through it. *It deals with torture,* Anna said. At one point Duras, a member of the Resistance, is in the room with a collaborator, a Frenchman accused of feeding secrets to the Nazis. As Duras tells it, she tortures this man—whether to get information or revenge or just because she can, I'm unsure. Granted, this was before the Geneva Conventions banned all torture, but where do I put it? Duras, a writer who saw me through my difficult early twenties, now reveals herself, without apology, as a torturer.

I didn't know it at the time, but this would be the last time Anna and I would ever speak. Maybe Anna knew, because she chose that moment to confess something—*I think I'm a drunk,* she said. Over the past two years, she told me, after we'd part, when we didn't know when we'd see each other again, she'd sometimes drink herself into oblivion. At night, after we hung up the phone, when we couldn't be together, not fully, or after I left, she'd take a few shots, wander down to some desolate patch of train tracks. *Pain devil,* she'd mutter, *leave me in peace.*

It may be hard to understand, but that Anna was drinking, that she ever drank, was not something I knew, not consciously. In my presence she'd never so much as take a sip, though I wouldn't have cared if she did. My family had all, to varying degrees, drowned themselves in alcohol—father, mother, grandmother, grandfather—I carry the weight of what alcohol has done to my family (or, more accurately, what my family has done to themselves with alcohol)—some days lightly, some days less so—but I have nothing against drinkers. Anna knew this, which is why her words were a revelation, a light turned on in a dark room. If it was true, if she was a *drunk,* if she drank alone, in secret, then it might go toward explaining the inexplicable distance I'd always felt, the unnamed shadow, hovering between us. Her confession was a light turned on in outerspace, and even then, as we tried to say goodbye, again, as our bodies floated over each other like doomed astronauts, those few words—*I think I'm a drunk*—connected us like tubes of oxygen.

dear reader (oblivion)

I bought my ticket, I got on this train, it seemed like I had some place to be. The train, at some point, went into a tunnel, one by one each car entered the hole dynamited clean through the mountain. It sounded like someone shuffling a deck of cards, it sounded like when the projectionist falls asleep before reel one ends, the acetate slapping the lens. As the train entered the mountain some part of me knew it would emerge again, in a few seconds or a few minutes, but once inside that tunnel I no longer cared if I ever came out the other side. In that darkness I felt held, I didn't want it to end. If the train broke down, if it stranded me in the darkness, I'd be blameless, like when I was a child, coming home from the drive-in, my mother steering us through the night, with me curled up in the backseat, lost in my kingdom of sleep. I could have stayed like that forever—my mother at the wheel, the radio softly playing, Laura Nyro or the Standells or Bobby Bland. I can open my eyes, even now, and she will be there, we will still be together, passing through dark streets—shadows of trees, shadows of telephone lines, breaking up the sky above us. When we pull into our driveway she will carry me inside, put me into bed, either hers or my own. I can't argue, maybe it's true, maybe I spent too many nights in her bed, trying to hold her to this earth, to quiet that voice inside her, calling her back from the darkness. Sometimes she'd go toward it, sometimes she'd get into her car after midnight, I'd hear it start up, I'd hear her pulling out, and later I'd hear her pulling back in, the gravel under her wheels.

I don't know how it is for you, but sometimes still I walk through my days, fighting the urge. Sometimes still I go on a little run, after so many years of being clean. I take a hit, I make a call. I knock on a door, someone answers, seemingly happy to see me. I say *Yes* and *yes* and *yes*. I say, *Why not?* I say, *Stay, the bed is huge, we can share it.* I take a hit, make a call, a month goes by, I take another, then maybe I take a hit every night for a month—nothing much, a fistful of marijuana, and then I don't pick up for a year. Then I call you from the bathtub, we make a plan. Then I hang up and call someone else.

What I'm trying to say is that one December day I reached the age my mother had been when she passed into nonbeing (*goodnight nobody, goodnight mush*), when she finally stepped through the door she'd had her hand on all those years. I don't know, maybe some part of me decided I should try to find her— she couldn't have simply vanished. And so, after years without drugs, I took a hit. Then I took another. I was alone in Sleepy Hollow, it was always after midnight, maybe some part of me believed it was the only way I could find my way back to her, but I didn't know it at the time—it's not something I could have *ar-tic-u-la-ted*. Others speak of the fireworks that come, once they fall off the wagon—the police at the door, the four-point restraint—but I use the same way my mother did. For both of us there were no fireworks. A glass of wine, a tiny pill, the flame to the pipe, whatever we did, however we did it, it merely eased us into the night, into our private oblivion, our quiet desperation. We both always had jobs to go to the next day, we both felt bad at the idea of just not showing up. We always showed up, until one day she just didn't.

Maybe what I'm trying to say is that Anna's words—*I think I'm a drunk*—made me realize that I hadn't been so clean myself. Before that moment, if anyone asked, I'd say that I hadn't had a drink in years, which was true, but I'd add that I sometimes took a hit of pot. I wasn't pretending to be sober, not exactly, but I wasn't saying I was out again either—I was *min-i-mizing* it. Then, after two years of getting high again, off and on, the voice inside began to murmur, softly at first, almost like an echo off a distant cliff, that everything would be better if I were dead. The suffering, my own and the suffering I was causing, would end. Step by step, inch by inch, hit by hit, lie by lie, slowly I turned. I brought myself to her door (my mother's? Anna's?), I put my hand upon it, a voice just on the other side, all I had to do was push it open, step through. I knew I would meet her there. I knew we could stay like that forever.

~

A few minutes or a few months after my mother died, my *Paradise Lost* professor ran into me one afternoon, putting gas into my motorcycle. I might have been on my way out of town, it might have been the last day I set foot on that campus. *Ah, it's nice to see you up on your steed again*, she said. I smiled. I liked her, I was sorry I'd stopped showing up for her class. *I'm doing a lot better*, I said. I looked at my motorcycle—*Lost*, I thought, *that's the name of my fucken steed*. I was fueling up, I was on my way, I would spend the next few lifetimes seeking it out. It isn't hard to get there—one left turn, down the end of the alley, down the cellar steps, knock on a door after midnight, your then-lover already in bed, waiting. The dragon is not dead, merely subdued beneath the hoof, beneath the tip of the lance. Two dogs live inside us. Say yes and yes and yes.

roulette

My grandmother does have one story she tells about her road-trip to Mexico, though she never mentions my grandfather when she tells it. She was walking down a village street, the village in the shadow of a volcano, and a boy came running up to her, a ball of hot lava in his hands. The boy shaped the lava into a monkey right there in front of her, then held it out to her. It sits now on a shelf in her kitchen, this small lava monkey, it's been there forever. She takes it down and works it with her hands whenever she tells this story, as if it were still warm, as if she could still transform it.

~

(2005) That spark I'd felt with Inez, our first night together, the glimmer that we could have a child together, was still flickering, but it was having a hard time finding purchase inside me. It felt unfamiliar, scattershot, it would flare up, at times, depending upon who I was with. Anna. Inez. At some point, after a year of being paralyzed, of being unable to choose, in what I now see as a sort of bottom, a sort of madness, I decided that whichever one got pregnant first would be the one I'd end up with—roll the dice. I would like to say that as soon as I heard this voice in my head I knew it was wrong, that I knew it was a very bad idea, that I saw how deeply I was lost, but that would not be true. This bad idea rumbled around inside me for months, it would flare up at times, seem perfectly reasonable, and then fade, but only for a while. Finally, dimly (starkly?) aware of how unquiet my mind had become, and starkly (dimly?) aware of how those around me were suffering, I committed to meditating every day for half an hour. I did this every day for almost two years, and once my mind had cleared, Anna and I were no longer in touch. In some ways, it seemed, Anna had only ever known my shadow, because that's all I'd been able to offer her.

nine

three dreams
(before the baby comes)

1.

I'm in a beach house, kissing a blond woman I don't
know very well. I get up from the bed and begin running swiftly down the beach, toward another woman.
Three dogs begin to chase me, and they catch up, and
one bites onto one hand, one onto the other, and one
bites my ass. I keep running, trying to shake them off,
but it hurts. The dogs' owner, a third woman, comes
over and tells me not to worry, that they won't hurt me.
I look at my hands and see that the dogs' teeth haven't
broken the skin. This woman leads me up a path and
we talk, but I can't remember about what. I end up in
a bar, and the woman I was making out with is now
bartending—in the harsh light I can see that her face is
very pockmarked.

2.

I am looking for Anna, who lives on a boat in a pro-
tected harbor. I stow away aboard a schooner, and we
sail around for a while. The others on the boat ignore
me, speak as if I am not there. When we sail near to

Anna's boat I jump onto it, then wander from cabin to cabin, but no one is inside. The trashbarrel under her galley sink is full, so I take out the bag and tie it up. In the bottom of the barrel is a black notebook, which has the words "Black Betty" in gold scroll on the cover. I hope to find some words inside, but inside all the pages are black. This disappoints me, but then I notice that each page is made of very fine silk. It feels incredible to touch them.

3.

Inez and I are trapped in a fascist country, and something bad is about to happen—arrest? I pay a man fifty dollars to get us out, across the border, but instead he takes us to a warehouse, and we end up in a room with a torturer, who takes Inez into the next room and begins raping her. I can see them from where I am, but I can't get to them—the man who brought us there blocks my way. This man, it becomes clear, is going to rape me as well. I get my hands on a gun, kill the first man, then I go into the next room and begin to torture the torturer—I shoot him in the knee, I shoot off his hand. Then I bring his son into the room and shoot him in the leg as well. I have become a monster.

too loud a solitude

(2006) June. Back north from Texas for the summer, I spend two days in Boston, cleaning out my father's studio apartment while Inez distracts him, playing Fay Wray to his King Kong. He has been in this apartment for the past sixteen years, since he got off the streets. Inez takes him to lunch, walks him around the block, listens to the same stories I've heard a hundred times before, all to keep him occupied while I drag trashbag after trashbag of his clutter down to the basement. I never wanted any of my friends to meet him, but a year ago I ran out of options. Verging on eviction, once again, and even Eileen, his saintly caseworker, says he'll be shit out of luck if he loses this place—*Nowhere will take in someone who drinks like he does.* If he loses this apartment he will be back out on the streets. *I'm Irish and Russian,* he reminds us, *I'd be insane not to drink.*

It's been a long year with my father. The landlord has been calling me, warning that his apartment has become a fire hazard, and I can't argue with this. My father, besides being an alcoholic, is also a hoarder—a not uncommon tick for the formerly homeless. But after sixteen years it has become nearly impossible to even open his door—every inch of floor space is stacked with newspapers, some of the stacks over six teetering feet high, leaving only narrow passageways from his bed to his bathroom, from his bed to his kitchen sink, which lately is overflowing with black, fetid water. *Something has to be done*, the landlord, a decent enough woman, warns me.

So here we are. I ring his bell (the bell with my last name still taped to it), he buzzes us in. I introduce Inez to him again, as his memory of her has been erased since our last visit, a couple months earlier. *Inez?* he asks. *A pleasure to meet you.* The plan is to invite him out to lunch, but on the way there I'll tell him that I've suddenly remembered something I have to do, suggest they go on ahead, that I'll meet up with them later. Then I'll let myself back into his apartment, a box of heavy-duty trashbags in my backpack. At the mention of lunch he perks up and puts on his jacket.

His collection of newspapers dates back to the first Bush presidency—his "research materials." Perhaps they once were, but I know he hasn't written a word in years. Ten years ago, maybe, we could have moved it all into storage, into a "unit," and he could have sold his blood to pay the rent on it, if it came to that. But he no longer has that option—at this point no one wants his blood, and, besides, he has refused to let go of a single yellowed headline. *This is my property*, he hisses. If he gets himself evicted he's too old, too frail, to survive another winter outside. I've gotten too old to survive it either, not knowing where he is, wondering if he'll make it through the night, looking up at the sky, wondering if it might snow. I'd hoped, for some unfathomable reason, that I could reason with him, that I could get him to take the looming eviction seriously, but it wasn't so. He threatened to kill himself, he threatened to kill the landlord, he threatened to kill me. After months of trying to reason with him, after the eviction notice had been filed, I spent two days with him, going through one small pile of newspaper, sheet by sheet, and we ended up getting rid of one small bag. It would take thirty years, at that rate, and we only had thirty days. And so I was forced to ask for help. And so here I am, sneaking back in while Inez distracts him.

Since January, I've hauled out sixty contractor bags. Yesterday I also dragged out a wing chair, the seat of which had collapsed under sixteen years of newspaper. I also cleaned out his kitchen sink, the toxic spore breeding ground—I've been soaking my infected finger in saline solution since.

In the months since January, I've called a lawyer, the mayor's office, his caseworker, anyone who might be able to help. A doctor I knew from my days of working with the homeless—Jim— came to my father's apartment, took his vitals. Jim arranged for my father to have a full checkup, so I brought him into the hospital a few weeks later. It turned out he was in better shape than I was—low blood pressure, low cholesterol, perfect liver function. How could this be?

Nothing I do, in the end, will keep my father inside. By stuffing the contractor bags without his consent, I settled the fire hazard issue, but in a few months he will wander into his landlord's office, threaten to murder everyone, including a seven-year-old black boy sitting in the waiting room with his mother. The landlord will call the police, and when she does, my father will threaten to cut his own throat, which the landlord knows by now is an idle threat, but the police overhear him, and they have to take such a threat seriously, and they do. They come, put him in restraints, and have him committed to a psych hospital for an evaluation.

When I finally broke down, when I finally asked for help, it was there—Inez, Jim, Eileen—it was as if everyone had been there all along, waiting for me to ask. If I'd been able to ask Anna for help I know she would have come, but I didn't ask her.

lexington, kentucky

When I'd see my father, those last few months, desperate to keep him from homelessness, again, I was unsure if he knew who I was. From moment to moment, it seemed, I'd fade in and out of focus. When I'd try to explain the urgency of his immanent eviction he'd interrupt me—*Dryballs*, he'd yell, *Will you let me speak!* "Dryballs"—this was new, this was a twist. It had its desired effect, at least the first dozen times he used it, in that I'd stand before him, completely unnerved—I didn't, after all, have a child at this point. *Will you let me speak!* And then he'd launch into one of the handful of stories that I've heard a hundred times before, sometimes the one about his time in federal prison:

> They left me alone in a dark room for days on end, shackled to the floor, and when they moved me, which they did constantly, and for no reason, they shackled me even more—penis included.

I didn't want to imagine how one shackles a penis, let alone my father's, which I didn't want to imagine at all.

Over the year of trying to keep my father inside, after I'd ransack his apartment for a couple hours, I'd meet him and Inez in the park or at a restaurant. Then we'd walk him back to his apartment, see if he'd notice what was no longer there. He'd look around his room furiously for a moment or two, and then let it go, as if some part of him knew we were just trying to help. As we'd prepare to leave, my father would turn to Inez—who he took to calling "Buttercup"—gesture toward her. *Are you leaving the woman?* he'd ask hopefully. *Are you leaving Buttercup with me?*

~

(2006) A historian is on the radio, talking about the history of the CIA's fifty-year involvement in developing the torture techniques we saw enacted in the Abu Ghraib photographs. The most effective technique, they found, was to combine sensory deprivation with self-inflicted pain *(the so-called light methods)*—think of the now-iconic photograph of the man on the box, hooded, his arms outstretched. This technique is not new, and it certainly wasn't invented by a few rogue nitwits on the night shift. It's a highly sophisticated stress position, developed, with the aid of the CIA, during Brazil's dirty war, and is known, among the professionals, as "The Vietnam." These days, when Iraqis pass around the photograph of the man on the box, they simply refer to it as "the Statue of Liberty."

At one point in the interview McCoy mentions the medical wings of federal prisons as the sites of early experimentation. Apparently the CIA used federal prisoners to test the limits of what the body, the psyche, could withstand. Two of the main sites of these clandestine and illegal experiments were the prisons in Lexington, Kentucky, and Marion, Illinois, both of which my father passed through during his stint behind bars.

I'll be damned.

Still, no Ishmael has come forward (not yet) to say, *Yes, I was there, I was with him, what your father says is true*. I have not found that person, if he even exists, who was strapped into the bed next to my father in the medical wing of Marion Federal Prison. I have not found anyone who can say that they heard my father scream, or saw him chained. I have not found a document with his name on it, numbers written into the margins—how long he was kept awake, how long he was made to kneel, how cold the cell was at night. All I have is a paranoid old man, who somehow tells the same stories I now hear on the radio.

the gulag archipelago

For years my father (the self-proclaimed *greatest-writer-America-has-yet-produced*) has compared himself to Solzhenitsyn, first in the letters he sent me from prison, and now face-to-face—*Solzhenitsyn will be green with envy when he reads this shit*, my father says, thumbing his unpublished manuscript.

Solzhenitsyn was arrested in the Soviet Union in 1945 for writing a derogatory comment in a letter to a friend. Accused of anti-Soviet propaganda under Article 58, he was sentenced to eight years in the gulag. My father, arrested in 1976 for passing forged checks, was sentenced to three-to-five years. Solzhenitsyn's books on his time in prison include *The Cancer Ward* and *The Gulag Archipelago*. In *The Gulag Archipelago* he writes:

> . . . *they gave precedence to the so-called light methods (we will see what they were immediately). This way was sure. Indeed, the actual boundaries of human equilibrium are very narrow, and it is not really necessary to use a rack or hot coals to drive the average human being out of his mind.*

You might wonder, perhaps, if my father got confused reading Solzhenitsyn, confusing whatever he went through in prison with what Solzhenitsyn went through. It's certainly possible that my father read Solzhenitsyn's accounts and transposed himself into his skin, his chair, his chains. But the secret history of the CIA's experiments on federal prisoners begs the question—did someone at the CIA also read *The Gulag Archipelago* and think, *Ah, the key?* Solzhenitsyn spends three pages documenting the various tortures he was subjected to, and concluded that these "light" methods (sensory deprivation, prolonged standing, extremes of temperature, forced sleeplessness) were the most effective, at least at breaking one's will and causing long-term damage. The CIA, it seems, came to the same conclusions. Yet Solzhenitsyn's account of life in the Soviet gulags were his way of dragging into the light what had happened to him, in part so it would never happen again. As for his tormenters he writes:

> But let us be generous. We will not shoot them. We will not pour salt water into them, nor bury them in bedbugs, nor bridle them into a "swan dive," nor keep them on sleepless "stand-up" for a week, nor kick them with jackboots, nor beat them with rubber truncheons, nor squeeze their skulls in iron rings, nor push them into a cell so that they lie atop one another like pieces of baggage—we will not do any of the things they did! But for the sake of our country and our children we have the duty to seek them all out and bring them all to trial! Not to put them on trial so much as their crimes. And to compel each one of them to announce loudly:
>
> "Yes, I was an executioner and a murderer."

Solzhenitsyn's point seems to have been lost, at least on some— his book has been used, by some, as more of a blueprint than a warning.

my augean stables

(2007) When—if—my father is finally released (banished?) from the psych hospital, it is unclear whether he will be able to return to his apartment. The landlord has grown tired of him, the neighbors have all complained. *I'm sorry,* his caseworker tells me, by phone. *He reeks of piss every time I see him. He's more belligerent, more out of control.* She sighs. *I've tried everywhere. Nobody will take him.* I hear exhaustion in her voice. *He has no options.*

What she's actually saying, I think, is that he has two options—either back on the streets, or move in with me, neither of which I'm ready to fully take in. *I hear he's been on meds in the psych ward,* I tell her, *that they've made him somewhat more docile. What if he stays on his meds,* I ask, *what if we find a pill that can calm him the fuck down?* Eileen considers this. *I couldn't go there everyday and give it to him,* she says, *and I don't know who could.* I look around my house, try to imagine my father rattling around these rooms. *Maybe once a week,* I offer, *maybe we could get one of those little pill boxes, the seven-day ones, and once a week you or me or someone goes in and doles out his pill, and we put up a little sign over his bed, or on his mirror, that says,* TAKE YOUR PILL, *and we get someone to come in once a week and hose him down, isn't there someone like that, that could make sure he showers, make sure he takes his pills, at least once a week?* I feel like I'm not breathing.

Well, we could maybe hook him up with a home health care person,
Eileen admits. *We could try that,* she says, but, really, she sounds
even less hopeful.

Which is why I'm on this train from New York to Boston,
for one last push to clean out his apartment. The plan is to hun-
ker down until I can clear out what still remains—the three
hundred pounds of moldy clothes that have lived in his bathtub
since I first came to see him ten years ago, his kitchen cabinets
crammed with uneaten food, the towers of magazines blocking access to his refrigerator. I'll pack his collection of metal
geegaws and piles of unfinished manuscripts and framed photographs of famous strangers (along with one of me as an infant
in his arms) into a few boxes, so that one day someone, nurse or
saint, might be able to enter, hose him down, hand him a pill.

Two days later, it's all gone—his entire apartment, his entire
life, now in boxes. All his writing, all his photos, packed up, the
rest of it dragged to the trash room in the basement. If, some-
day, he wants what I've salvaged, if he remembers, if he misses
it, I will bring these boxes to him. But I know, deep down, that
he's never coming back, to this or to any apartment. As it turns
out, this is a one-way trip—he will be transferred from the
psych ward to a rehab unit to a long-term care facility. From
blood tests it will turn out that he's had some kind of stroke in
the past year—he's incontinent, his mind is shot, he's no longer
able to live on his own. I don't know this when I am cleaning
out his apartment, but I will come to accept it, a month or so
later, after I talk to Eileen and his doctor.

~

In the midst of transitioning my father into his new life, Inez and I decide to have a child together. Or, at least, we decide to try. It's a leap, for both of us, empty-handed into the unknown. For me, maybe the time I spent with my father these last several years, maybe the days I spent in his apartment these last few weeks, on my hands and knees, dealing with his detritus, maybe it made me see how everything one collects over the course of one's life turns to dust, in the end. Even the book you spend your whole life writing will one day end up in a box, if you're lucky, or on the sidewalk, if you're not. I'd spent so much time, so many years, trying to prop my father up, trying to keep him from dying on the streets, I can't even say why, any more than a salmon could tell you why it needed to return to the river where it had been conceived. Maybe it was some combination of these forces, of seeing how a life can fall apart, alongside the animal instinct to hold it all together, maybe this had something to do with deciding that now, with Inez, I could try to have a child. Maybe it was that I'd asked for her help and she'd been there, maybe it was simply that some part of me knew it would be alright. Maybe some part of me knew Inez would be a good mother, and that Inez and I could figure a way around whatever obstacle we came upon. Still, though, part of me felt like when I was a teenager, standing on a bridge on a summer day, getting ready to dive into the river below. Back then I'd discovered that the whole trick was to simply take one step into the air, then let gravity take over. The whole trick was to become disembodied, but that trick no longer worked, not as well as it once had.

Whatever my reasons, after those final two days of trying to make my father's apartment more human, I needed to return to New York, because now my presence was required on a certain day each month. The day was upon us. I'm not talking about it much, in case it doesn't work out, so as not to make it too real, but I do tell my friend Philip. Philip has three kids of his own.

Trying? he smiles. *Enjoy the ride.*

Back home, my car crammed with my father's boxes, a pile of unopened mail waits on my dining room table—bills to be paid, books to be commented on. At this moment I don't know when—if—I will get to any of it. I send an email to my pal Sarah:

> . . . *my old man got committed to a psych ward last week. I had to make two trips to Boston to finish the emptying of his apartment, on my hands and knees in an inch of spilt soil from long-dead plants, the dirt soaked with piss, the toilet smeared with shit, sweeping up dead rodents, along with three crack pipes (a crack whore—"Fancy Nancy"—would stay with him at the beginning of each month, help him spend his Social Security check), and hundreds of bright green rat poison pellets. Twenty-year-old newspapers were stuck to the carpet, in dust thick with cackling faces. I did it in the deluded hope that if his apartment is more human he won't live like such an animal, that he might be able to stay off the streets, for at least another winter. I want him to enter his apartment on some magic happy pill and forget the way he has lived his whole life. I want him to forget all those years he's been living in his own dirt, what's that song? like a monkey in a zoo. . . .*

I'd taken a few books for myself from his apartment, including a copy of *The Big Book* from Alcoholics Anonymous, one of
several that people had apparently, and to little effect, put into
his hands over the years. I also took his worn copy of *The Gulag
Archipelago*—*And it turned out that each of us had been imprisoned
for nothing much.*

ten

two strong men

My dharma teacher relates a story the Buddha told about a boy who lived in a small village, and on the edge of his village was a huge pit filled with burning coals. It troubled the boy, this pit, the idea that he might one day wander too close, fall in. And so the boy leaves his village, begins his life as a wanderer. This is the Chinese version of the story, the teacher tells us, but in the Indian version the boy, before he can leave the village, finds himself one day being dragged toward the pit by two strong men. We are left to assume that they either throw him in or else he escapes. The two strong men might be our desires, the teacher tells us, and to be aware of our desires can sometimes be enough.

~

(2007) Inez is two months pregnant. I bike into the city one night to give a reading at a New York bar called KGB. Afterward a young woman comes up to me, holds out her closed hand, asks if it's okay if she gives me a gift. We'd never met before, but she'd seen something in a store just before the reading, and thought of me. When she opened her hand, there in her palm was a small bronze statue of a monkey, standing on his hind legs, his two hands clasping his chest. Only he wasn't merely pointing to his heart, like Jesus—he was ripping his chest open. *I saw it and thought of you*, she said (in one of my poems Jesus rips open his shirt to show us his heart, *all flaming & thorny*). Not even as long as my pinkie, I recognized him as a Hindu god, but I couldn't remember his name. *What's his name?* I asked. Inside his open chest I can see a tiny heart.

A few days later I look it up: the monkey god is Hanuman— *The planets are under control of Hanuman's tail, and whoever worships him is granted fortitude and strength.* The girl who held her hand out to me, offering me this tiny god, was very beautiful. *Fortitude, strength*—can I say I didn't want this girl to take me home with her? Can I say it doesn't pass through my mind now? But if she were to appear before me, which version of me would she find?

lisbon

(1986) After two years of working in the shelter, I decide I need to take a winter off. I fly to Europe and end up spending six months wandering, first in Paris, where I find a squat for two months, and then I push on, first to Spain, then into Portugal, then on to Morocco. By the end, on the edge of the Sahara, part of me wants to just keep going, to never go back home. I couldn't know it at the time, but after I return to Boston, within a year of being back to work at the shelter, my father will show up at the door, and he will end up sleeping there, off and on, for the next five years.

In Lisbon, my first day there, I meet a woman—Carmo—and end up staying with her for a month, helping her to renovate her apartment. Lisbon had only recently emerged from its totalitarian nightmare, and it still seemed suitably gritty, which is how I like my cities—if there's still some grit it seems they can absorb a wider range of people, not just the rich. One day I took a train with Carmo north, to the town of Sintra, where she had to appear in court to clear up a minor traffic violation. While waiting for her in the hallway outside the courtroom, shafts of sunlight streamed through the dusty Gothic windows, both illuminating and enshrouding the few people awaiting their turn before the judge. I took my camera out, snapped a picture. As I put the camera down, I noticed that one of the people in the hallway was wearing a uniform, and that he was now walking toward me. I put my camera back in my bag. This soldier stopped directly in front of me, blocking my way, though I wasn't attempting to go anywhere. Half a foot shorter than I was, he whispered something menacing into my face that I didn't understand. *Sorry*, I said, *I'm just a tourist, no problem*, hoping Carmo would appear and translate my way out of whatever was happening. But she didn't, and the soldier took my arm and directed me toward a door. Once we passed through it we were in another hallway, where six or seven men had on the same uniform. The small soldier put his face close to mine and murmured *Pelicula, pelicula, pelicula*, which I understood was the word for film, as I had just bought some earlier that day. He gestured for me to hand it over. *Just a snapshot*, I said, *just a tourist, no problem*, and that was when he punched me in the stomach. It didn't hurt, not as much as you might think—it was more of a shock. I looked around at the other soldiers— some looked at their shoes, some smoked their cigarettes, some smiled and looked away. I held up my hand. *No problem*, I said, and reached into my bag and took the camera out. As I did he punched me again, in the same spot, the spot the doctor had pulled my spleen out of a few years back. This time the whole thing was more of a dance—he leaned into it more, I rounded my back, pushed my weight up on my toes, absorbed it. The sentence, *I am far from home and getting beaten up by a soldier*, ran through my mind. I now had the camera in one hand—*Pelicula*, he hissed, gesturing, and I started to rewind the film—I didn't want to open the camera to the light and ruin the whole roll. When done I popped the camera open and handed him the roll, and as he held it in one hand he punched me one last time. After that it seemed we were finished, so I pushed my way past him, back out through the door. Carmo was in the hallway, wondering where I'd been. Shaky, I explained quickly that I'd lost the film, and that we should leave immediately, before the door opened again. Unfortunately, on the same roll were some photographs documenting the work we'd been doing on her apartment, and she needed these photographs to get reimbursed by her landlord. So she knocked on the door, and the little soldier came out, and she explained the situation, but he refused to give us back the film. My friend asked to speak to his commanding officer, and soon we were outside, talking to a little general in a little jeep, which is how it is that I have a photograph of the soldier who punched me three times in the stomach. It is the other soldiers, though, the soldiers outside of the photo, the ones who merely smiled and looked away, that now trouble me more.

locusts

(1968) When I was eight my family flew to Montana to stay with my uncle's family—my mother's brother and my aunt and cousins who, in the way of our family, I barely knew. Two things from that trip stay with me—first was the locusts, which that summer filled the sky with their frenzy. During the day the cousins and I built tiny Lego cells in the driveway, which we filled with locusts, and then we'd watch with our own increasing frenzy as they ripped each other apart. The air was thick with them—at one point we took a road trip to Glacier National Park and had to stop at every gas station, to clear their splattered corpses from the windshield.

The other thing I remember from Montana is coming home from Glacier, stopping at a "trading post," the kind of place that sold turquoise bolo ties and rubber tomahawks. It also had a few animals in cages out back—ROADSIDE ZOO—a handpainted arrow pointing the way. The animals were kept in tiny cinderblock cages, and the one I remember was the bald eagle, which could barely lift its head as I fluttered my hands before the bars.

a trail of breadcrumbs

(1969) A neighbor of my grandmother is carried out of her house on a stretcher, the stretcher covered with a white sheet, a blossom of red where her head should be. To get here I'd cut through some scraggly woods at the edge of my grandmother's lawn, then ran across Kent Street. The house is a run-down place perched on the marsh, teetering on the lowlands. When I'd heard the sirens I did what my mother had taught me—I followed the sound, I stood on the sidewalk, I waited.

Later that night, when I asked what had happened, my mother told me that the woman had been sitting at her kitchen table, and that she'd asked her two sons to help her with something—peeling apples, I imagined. I imagined she was baking a pie, like my mother did.

Do it yourself, one son answered.

I'm busy, said the other son.

These sons were delinquents, my mother explained, causing their mother no end of heartache. *I'm sick of this,* the woman said, putting down her apple or her rolling pin. *I can't take your ungratefulness.* And then she reached into a drawer and pulled out her gun and put it on the table.

I'm going to kill myself, she said.

Go ahead, said the first son.
You wouldn't dare, said the second.

~

Go ahead—it would take me years to realize that there was really no way my mother could have known the details of that conversation around that kitchen table, not then, if ever. Years later, in therapy, I remembered that as an even younger child I'd said the same thing to my mother, one snowy night, as I ran around the house naked, refusing to get dressed for bed. My mother had threatened to throw me outside in the snow if I didn't do as she said. I answered, *You wouldn't dare,* the thrill of a strange new power surging through me. She grabbed me and tossed me out onto the front porch. I stood there for a few seconds, shivering, trying to cover my nakedness, then I ran and hid behind the stone wall in the neighbor's yard, the same place I'd stood just the year before, the night I watched the shadows of flames dance across the face of our house.

heroic uses of concrete

I never wanted to attach the name "addiction" to my mother's suicide, I never wanted to allow something as tiny as a pill that power. Sometimes, if asked, I'd say it was a bullet, and sometimes I'd say it was confusion. Sometimes I'd say she'd worked too hard her whole life, and sometimes I'd say that raising two kids alone had worn her out. I looked up the word "suicide" in the dictionary after she died, and one definition said that suicide was an act of a sane mind: *suicide* (n.) 1. the act of killing oneself intentionally; in law, the act of self-destruction by a person sound in mind and capable of measuring his moral responsibility. I carried that definition around for years, as if some part of me needed to believe that what she'd done was an act of clarity. After I quit drinking—before my slip—I would sometimes call her an "addict," but I never really believed it, not deeply. Her suicide had to have been caused by something more than what could be corked in a bottle or folded into tinfoil—nothing so small, so insignificant, could have taken her. You know how it is, how we don't want to believe that Lee Harvey Oswald could have acted alone, how we don't want to believe that a handful of maniacs with boxcutters could have taken down our towers. Our fear is so big, so real, that we want what we fear to be something formidable, not some skinny psychopath, not some misfits living in caves. Not our own shadows.

Here, then, is one last fact:

My mother took her life two weeks before her gangster boy-friend was to be released from prison—he was finishing up two years of a three-to-five-year federal sentence. A few years earlier we'd seen him on the evening news, in handcuffs, being led off a boat laden with marijuana. While the gangster had been locked up, my mother had gotten together with another man. I knew that part of her was tormented by that, by what she would do the moment when, if, they were all face-to-face. Call it guilt. Call it confusion. Call it monkey-mind. Call it samsara when, years later, I'm in love with two women, and suffocating under the weight of it all.

the navigator (goodbye)

The Navigator is a silent film about a man adrift on a large ship in the middle of the sea. Buster Keaton plays a rich man—lost in the way only the rich can be lost—who, until the moment he finds himself alone on this luxury liner, has had everything done for him. If I am remembering it correctly, Keaton had his chauffeur drive him to the ship for a gala, but he was a day early and the ship was empty—imagine the *Queen Mary* without captain, without crew, the deck chairs all lined up and empty. Keaton wanders the decks for a while, looking for the party, and ends up falling asleep in a stateroom. In the night the ship is cut loose from its dock, and he wakes up the next morning, no land in sight. Bewildered, he wanders the decks, looking first for everyone, then for anyone. In one scene he finds a can of food in the galley, and he spends a long time pondering it—he has never had to open a can. Eventually he puts the can in a vice and takes a fire axe to it. I don't remember if he ever finds his way inside this can.

~

(2007) After I've stopped using (again), after I've found my way back into folding chairs in anonymous church basements, after

a year and a half of not hearing from her, five months into Inez's pregnancy, Anna sends this note:

> *I just woke up from a long night of dreaming about you: in the last dream, I was trying to get you to say goodbye to me, as I so often was in real life, and you instead were insisting we jump off a cliff with our pockets full of keys, a freefall. We jumped, and when we landed, we were separated, in rushing water, pockets empty. . . .*

numerology

(2008) It's two days past the due date for our child to appear. *Appear*—is that even the right word? Hasn't she been with us always, manifest, as the Buddhists say, like the flame in the match? Her due date was the fourth of January, the doctor told us months ago. We knew it was merely an approximation, more mathematics than gospel, but numerology, apparently, is a superstition I find hard to let go of—on the due date I was so full of energy that I could barely contain it.

~

Last night I had a dream—my friend David had built a huge boat out of cardboard, like the boat in *Fitzcarraldo*, or in *The Navigator*. We motor it out along a wide river that opens in the distance to the sea. David took the wheel first, and when it looked like we were heading into the shallows I went to the bow and lay on my belly, on the lookout for submerged rocks. As I watched the eel grass sway, my eyes got heavy, and though I tried to resist, I fell asleep. When I woke up, David was gone. I was alone, the boat drifting aimlessly, near to the shoals. I take the wheel, but it turns uselessly in my hands, so I drop anchor, and then I fall asleep again. When I awaken, the rising tide has pulled the anchor up, and so the boat is again adrift. I find a switch, which starts the engines, and this time I am able to steer away from the shoals. The dream went on like this all night— me falling asleep, waking up, drifting into danger, starting the engine, dropping anchor, safe for a moment in clear beautiful water, the eel grass swaying, until I drift off again, and wake up in danger.

~

For a long time after my mother died—ten years or so, off and on—I lived on a boat. When my father got himself evicted and ended up homeless, I was still on that boat, I still hadn't made my way to shore. My twenties, you could say, were water, you could say I was, in a way, more ocean than earth. You could say that whatever was solid in me was slowly dissolving. I had read somewhere that nothing should change after a *serious trauma*, in the face of *such a loss*. I was away at school when I got the call, but when I came home it was no longer my home. I dropped out of school but I never spent another night in that house. If I tried I'd wake up, hungover, slouched in the front seat of my car, the car itself sideways in the driveway. The boat was on land in a friend's yard, and I'd often go to it in the middle of the night, crawl aboard. We put her back in the water that spring.

~

In my late teens, working for the gangsters, I spent a year or so knee-deep in ice and fish slime in the holds of various fishing boats. *Hold*—like a child in her mother's belly, just before being born. Then she will be held in another way. It was my job to unload these boats, to shovel the icy corpses into a basket dangling off the dock from a winch. The DEA was filming us from nearby rooftops, but the boats laden with marijuana were being unloaded three hundred miles to the north, in Portland, Maine. Then, if it was that time of year, the kilos were packed onto the bottom of a flatbed truck, which was then loaded with Christmas trees and driven into the city—*ho-ho*. Now, two days after the due date, I bend down to Inez's belly and murmur, *We're waiting for you, little one, the coast is clear.*

eleven

piero della francesca

(2008) *I read the news today, oh boy*—over thirty thousand Iraqis are now detained in U.S.-built prisons, twice as many as were jailed at the time of the Abu Ghraib photos. And these are merely the ones we know about. This number includes women and children—at the time the Abu Ghraib photographs were taken we know that the youngest detainee was ten, kidnapped and held, the idea being to force his father to talk, though it is unlikely that his father had anything to say. It is now widely believed that no actionable intelligence ever came out of Abu Ghraib, and that even the U.S. military knew that 90 percent of those held were guilty of nothing. Which begs the question—why we are doing it, why did we open that box, shut for fifty years?

~

(1455) The title of one of Piero della Francesca's frescoes from the fifteenth century in the Basilica di San Francesco in Arezzo is *The Torture of the Jew*. The Jew, in this case, is named Judas, but is not the Judas who betrayed Jesus with that kiss. From the plaque beneath it we now learn that this Judas was lowered into a hole, a well, without food or water for six days, in order to coerce him into revealing the location of "the one true cross." A man in a blue tunic is in charge, his hand on Judas's head, though it's unclear if he's pushing Judas down or pulling him out. The man in blue holds a stick in his other hand, striped blue and white—it's the type of stick that would show the blood if he were forced to use it. Judas has one foot on the lip of the well, both hands brace his body, but, again, we don't know if he is stepping out after six days beneath the ground or if he is trying to keep from falling in. Judas appears well dressed, clean, so it wouldn't be unreasonable to imagine this is the beginning of his descent, the first moment, as it were—Judas at the threshold, Judas with his annunciating angels. Two men work a rope that is tied to Judas's waist, lowering or raising him from a wooden scaffold. With its precise rendering of knots and scaffold it is the equivalent of a how-to manual.

Piero della Francesca also painted more iconic depictions of torture, such as *The Flagellation of Jesus*, which hangs in the Galleria Nazionale delle Marche in Urbino. We have seen this flagellation portrayed before, it is one of the ways we know Jesus, through his suffering, which is sometimes called the Passion. The composition of this painting is classical, balanced. You could break it down into perfect triangles, talk about where the eye is led. Within this form there is the story—the two men who whip the bound Jesus are not asking him anything, they are not looking for an answer or for information, they are merely whipping him because of who he is or claims to be—the Son of God. A spray of blood hangs from both of Jesus' shoulders, like wings. His expression is calm, as if it is happening to someone else and he is looking on with pity.

the passion (misnamed)

(*2004*) A few months before the Abu Ghaib photographs are leaked to the world, the film *The Passion of the Christ* is released. Human rights lawyers, and of course those in the military and those who make the rules for those in the military, already know what is going on in Abu Ghraib, as well as in all of the "black sites" around the world. The gloves have come off, we've been told, and we know what this means. I'm in Texas when *The Passion* opens. The mega-churches send busloads of the faithful to pack the theaters, helping to make it the highest-grossing R-rated film of all time. It is rated R for its depiction of violence, which is relentless. Jesus spends nearly two hours being (almost) flayed. It is criticized, by some, for ignoring the central message of forgiveness in Jesus' teachings. It is still in the theaters when the Abu Ghraib photographs appear, and some read it as a justification, of sorts—*Look at what Jesus suffered for our sins, and you're worried about a little smacky-face?*

the lion of babylon

(2004) One story that circulated after the Abu Ghraib photographs appeared was that the Americans had used lions to intimidate and torture prisoners—one more small strange story in a clusterfuck of awful stories. The lion story, as I remember it, circulated on Arab websites, either because it had happened or merely as an allegory, to show the barbarity of the occupiers. In the West this story was used, by some, to show that nothing the former prisoners said could be taken seriously, or at least not without a healthy dose of skepticism—*lions in the prisons?* To some, this was clearly a fantasy taken straight from stories of the Crusades (our president, though, did refer to the invasion as a "crusade"), or from the history of Roman persecutions of Christians in the now-ruined Colosseum.

The more I look into it, though, the more I wonder. I come up with this list of three (possibly paranoid) questions:

— Is it possible that the source of this story isn't a former Iraqi prisoner at all, but part of a CIA campaign of disinformation, for in the end it is so incredible that it allows all claims of torture to be doubted?

— If you are forced to wear a hood and a soldier who
doesn't speak your language is siccing a dog on you,
maybe even allowing the dog to draw blood, is it
possible that the dog's growl could be mistaken for a
lion's growl?

— When we invaded Iraq in March 2003 there followed
several days, then years, of chaos—museums looted,
power plants dismantled, zoos neglected. What happened to the lions, assuming there were lions?

I type the words "lion torture iraq" into a search engine, and
discover this:

Former Iraqi Detainees Allege Torture

*ABC News has an exclusive report of two released Iraqi detainees
who allege shocking accounts of torture by U.S. troops. Aside
from physical beatings, the men allege:*

*"They took us to a cage—an animal cage that had lions
in it within the Republican Palace," he said. "And they
threatened us that if we did not confess, they would put us
inside the cage with the lions in it. It scared me a lot when
they got me close to the cage, and they threatened me. And
they opened the door and they threatened that if I did not
confess, that they were going to throw me inside the cage.
And as the lion was coming closer, they would pull me
back out and shut the door, and tell me, 'We will give you
one more chance to confess.' And I would say, 'Confess to
what?'"*

As it turns out, there were in fact quite a few lions in Iraq when we invaded. Saddam's son Uday kept several in his palace. It is alleged that he fed them on human meat, and that sometimes he even fed them live humans. As the search continues I find this:

> Coalition rockets and gunfire had nearly destroyed the palace grounds, and none of the troops expected to find anything alive. Then, in a small, war-scarred compound, Staff Sgt. Darren Swain peered into a room—and saw three lions, cowering, starving and abandoned.

After these lions were discovered, despite urgings by international aid organizations to relocate them to other more secure and humane zoos, they were kept in the palace. Finally, I stumble upon this bit of history:

> Meanwhile, in a deserted Babylon tormented by sandy winds, the Lion of Babylon is still standing: it has not been stolen or vandalized. The Lion of Babylon—supposedly a trophy from Hitite times, middle of the 2nd millennium B.C., when Nebechadnezzar was king—is an enigmatic basalt statue representing a man who is about to be killed by a lion. But in fact the man is resisting: with one hand he tries to shove the lion's mouth away, and with the other he fights one of the lion's menacing paws. Legend rules that as long as the statue is there, Babylon will never be conquered.

The Iraqis, it seems, have been fighting lions for a long time.

invasion of the body snatchers

At the end of Polanski's *Chinatown*, John Huston turns to Jack Nicholson—*But you see, Mr. Gittes, most people never have to face the fact—the right time, the right place, and they are capable of anything. . . .* In another favorite zombie movie of mine, the remake of *Invasion of the Body Snatchers*, Brooke Adams turns to Donald Sutherland as he drives her to the psychiatrist—*Yesterday it all seemed normal, today everything seemed the same but it wasn't.* Brooke didn't know, couldn't know, not then, that Donald was gone, already gone.

~

(1980) After the gangster my mother was dating got arrested, his crew figured out it was simpler to fly a few hundred pounds of cocaine in from Mexico than to sail back from Colombia in a boat laden with marijuana. They'd still do the occasional marijuana run, but cocaine brought in a lot more money, a lot quicker, though it also sped up the unraveling. The gangsters began using, which meant that my mother's boyfriend (before he was sentenced) began using, which meant that my mother began using. I began finding cut straws in her glove compartment—I'd imagine her sitting in her car in the bank parking lot, doing a

line or two at lunch, then going back in to finish counting out the money. I'd split the straws open to lick out the bitter residue. Around this time she began hanging with a woman named Karen, the girlfriend of one of the other gangsters, and the two of them would be over at our house some evenings, wild-eyed and loud, getting ready to go out. Karen was hard around the edges, missing a tooth in the front of her face—she looked like she'd been using for a while, certainly longer than my mother, who was only just beginning to show some wear, mostly just around her eyes.

a story that could be true

(2006) A photograph of Ali Shalal Qaissi appears on the front page of the *New York Times*. Qaissi, a gray-haired Iraqi, his head bowed, is holding in his hands one of the photographs from Abu Ghraib—that of the hooded man standing on the box. The caption identifies Mr. Qaissi as the man depicted in this infamous, now-iconic photograph. A powerful image, a photograph of a photograph, with the hood now removed so we can see, for the first time, his face. It seems to capture a rare combination of humility and bravery, for this man to publicly acknowledge himself as a survivor of torture. Yet, even more than this, it is powerful because so few Iraqi voices from that time, that place, have been heard.

The documentary filmmaker Errol Morris wrote a piece for the *New York Times* a year or so later about Mr. Qaissi (Morris refers to him throughout as "Clawman," the [demeaning] nickname given him by the MPs at Abu Ghraib):

> *The photograph of the Hooded Man has created its own iconography and its own narrative. Like the unknown soldier, there is something mysterious about an unknown victim. Who is the Hooded Man? The Times picture of Clawman provides not just*

an identification of the Hooded Man. It provides the solution
to a mystery. (A who-is-under-it, rather than a who-dunnit?)
The Times piece assumes that we know what happened to the
Hooded Man—the nature of the abuses he suffered—but if
Clawman isn't the Hooded Man, whose account are we listen-
ing to?

As it turned out, the *Times* had issued a retraction a week after
the photograph had appeared—the man on the box was not Mr.
Qaissi after all, but a man named Abdou Hussain Saad Faleh.
When pressed, Mr. Qaissi claimed to have been subjected to the
same treatment, to have been photographed in that same position, but acknowledged that it was possible that it was not him
in the *iconic* photograph. Morris continued:

> *The identity of the figure under the hood is actually known.*
> *His real name is Faleh, his nickname is Gilligan, but what is*
> *his story? What happened to him at Abu Ghraib?*

Yes, the story of what happened to Mr. Faleh is vital for us to
understand what happened at Abu Ghraib, but Mr. Faleh will
not be heard from—he vanished after being released from Abu
Ghraib, so we may never know his side of the story, beyond
a limited testimony he gave for the Taguba Report. Morris
continued:

> *Clawman was playing to an expected narrative of abuse. The*
> *story had been widely circulated. The wires, the threat of elec-*
> *trocution had become well known. But herein lies the circu-*
> *larity. We see the picture of the Hooded Man. We imagine the*

abuse. Quotes from Clawman in the accompanying text confirm
our worst suspicions about what happened at Abu Ghraib. Our
beliefs about the picture are confirmed—except that we know
nothing more than when we started. We have learned nothing.

Morris wrote this essay while working on his film *Standard Oper-*
ating Procedure, an examination of the Abu Ghraib photographs.
Morris has described his project as having a "narrow focus,"
intentionally limited to those portrayed in the photographs. I
appreciate the need to impose limits on oneself—the world is
vast, impossible to contain in one jar. Morris continues:

> *Another theory is that Clawman's story was not a hoax, that he*
> *believed it to be true and is innocent of conscious manipulation*
> *or misrepresentation. In this version, Clawman, like Gilligan,*
> *was put on a box with wires. And since he was hooded, he*
> *could have thought that he was the Hooded Man.*

Morris dismisses this possibility offhand, yet it doesn't seem so
far-fetched—Physicians for Human Rights examined Mr. Qaissi
in Amman, Jordan, in 2006, and corroborate his claims that he
was subjected to electroshock and beatings. And no one denies
that he was at Abu Ghraib at the time of the photographs—he
is, in fact, depicted, unhooded—in several other photographs.
Also, at least five photographs of hooded men on boxes came
out of Abu Ghraib, and some of these are clearly of different
men. One even appears to be missing two fingers from his left
hand, as does Mr. Qaissi. But Morris's "narrow focus" seems to
limit him to versions given by Americans, which gives credence
to one of the MPs depicted in several photographs, Sabrina Har-

man (of the thumbs-up-over-a-corpse fame), who may or may not be telling self-serving (or CIA-debriefed and -approved) versions of the events of those strange nights.

> *Sabrina Harman, an M.P. (who took several pictures of both Clawman and Gilligan), says: "No. Gilligan was on the box, not Clawman." Clawman was her prisoner, and according to her, he was not put on a box, nor attached to wires. She also said, "Clawman was heavy-set. Gilligan was short and slight. If Clawman had been put on a box, he would have crushed it."*

One problem with this assertion is that Harman spent a total of eleven days on tier 1A, so it would be impossible for her to say whether Mr. Qaissi was ever put on a box, let alone whether a box was ever found that could have held his weight. It is possible she didn't see him placed on a box in those eleven days, but she cannot say he was never placed on a box. Nor can she say that he is not one of the other hooded men balanced on a box in the other photographs.

The question I would have asked Harman was whether she was aware that this torture technique—a man forced to stand on a box, wired and hooded—has (as noted earlier) a name: *The Vietnam*, created by the CIA during Brazil's dirty war in the 1970s, which makes the likelihood that it was an isolated instance that just happened to be captured on film that much less credible. More credible is the possibility that, like Palestinian hangings, hoodings, nakedness, waterboarding and beatings, it was simply one of the approved "enhanced techniques" floating through those halls. Techniques authorized by the president, brought in by CIA ghosts and private contractors, implemented by soldiers who had come untethered. Morris, it seems, did not ask this question, focused as he was only on those (Americans) depicted in the photographs. His essay continues:

> One human rights worker suggested that it made no difference whether Clawman was really the Hooded Man—that his testimony was no less valid. I do not agree. Now we are talking about reality—not about photographs. Clawman was a prisoner at Abu Ghraib. He was most likely subjected to abuse, but whatever his account might be, it's not the account of the man in the picture. That man is Gilligan—not Clawman.

Morris seems to be suggesting that Mr. Qaissi appropriated someone else's (Faleh's) pain, cobbling together a narrative of abuse which may or may not be somewhat fictive. It is, of course, vital to get the stories right—something happened the night that Mr. Faleh was photographed on the box, but this in no way cancels out what happened on other nights, to other detainees. Unfortunately, if Morris (or his collaborator, Philip Gourevitch) spent much time tracking down these stories from the Iraqis themselves, they ended up on the cutting room floor. What we are left with are the voices of the MPs, who, either unfortunately or by choice, became torturers. Those on the wrong end of the leash, as it were, remain silent.

Morris, for his part, risks being known as the man who views Abu Ghraib as primarily a problem with getting the captions right, rather than a moral catastrophe.

twelve

electra

(2008) Labor came on gradually, five days after the due date. By then I'd almost convinced myself the wait could just go on and on. It started just after midnight, and we took a cab to the hospital the next afternoon. We were in the hospital for a total of seven hours, a hospital on the Upper East Side, where it was hard to find a nurse who'd been present for a natural childbirth, which Inez was hoping to attempt. Twenty hours into it she asked to be prepped for an epidural—the pain was mind-bending, too much, but by then it was too late. Inez breathed and moved through it, and the baby came just after midnight, twenty-four hours after labor began.

Outside there was snow on the ground.

In the days between the due date and the birth, I'd been reading Anne Carson's translation of *Electra*. In her introduction Carson breaks down the subtle nuances of Electra's screams. During the last two hours of labor, when I'd wander into the hallway for another cup of water, or just to catch my breath, the other nurses seemed huddled at their station, wide-eyed, listening to Inez's screams coming from our room at the end of the hall. All the other rooms on that floor, where many other children were being born, were in a drug-induced silence.

self-portrait as an infant
in my father's arms

Unuttered, but always present, was the fear that Inez would die in childbirth—don't women sometimes die in childbirth? Unuttered was the fear that the baby would be a miscarriage, or else not survive her first hours, her first days. Unuttered was the image I carried of myself after this disaster—wandering the face of the earth, unrecognized, barefoot, alone.

~

I have in my hand a photograph of my father sitting in a chair— I am the infant in his arms. We both look into the camera, or at least at whoever it is that is taking the photograph—my mother, I imagine, since I found it with her things. The look on his face is heavy, as if I were a burden, as if he were burdened, though perhaps I am simply reading into it, knowing that he will be gone in a few months—impossible not to read into it. How old am I? He was gone by the time I was six months old, or we were gone, my mother taking me, us, away. Choose a version, choose a victim. The look on his face is a tunnel, leading out—no one would call it happy.

And now I have a picture of me with my daughter in my arms, in almost the same pose, all these years later. Now I am older than my mother made it to, older than my father before he walked into that bank with his forged check, smiling into the camera. I have her in my arms, and I am smiling so broadly that I barely recognize myself.

Those first few moments, holding our newborn in that hospital room, I thought about my father, which surprised me. My father never made it to the hospital for either my brother's birth or mine, claiming car trouble both times (though he ran a car dealership). I'd never thought much about it, but as I held our newborn in my arms I felt sad for him, having chosen vodka (or did vodka choose him?) over this simple moment.

We didn't name her for three days, not until we were about to leave the hospital, until it was made clear to us that if we simple wrote BABY GIRL FLYNN on the birth certificate, as a placeholder, then this name would haunt her for the rest of her life. When she was thirty-five, a letter might come in the mail from some obscure bureaucracy, addressed to BABY GIRL FLYNN.

So we named her Maeve Lulu, after the Queen of the Fairies.

~

And now some weeks have passed, some sleepless weeks, and I am less certain about that photograph of me in my father's arms. Maybe he is simply tired, bone-tired. Maybe he's been up all night, trying to soothe me back to sleep, and what I see in his face is not unhappiness, only exhaustion. If you took a photograph of me one of these sleepless nights, pacing the apartment and singing *All you need is love* softly to Lulu, desperate for us both to return to the land of sleep, you might say that I don't look especially thrilled at this miracle I am holding in my arms. But you would be wrong. And so, maybe I've been wrong, all these years, about my father.

thirteen

the uses of enchantment (flying monkeys)

The scariest moment in *The Wizard of Oz* is, still, when the flying monkeys fill the sky, sent out by the Wicked Witch to hunt down Dorothy and her pals. It still surprises me, every time, how terrifying they are, the way they move, the way they hover over the earth, how they land running, folding their wings up onto their backs. The thing I always forget about the monkeys is that they're under some sort of spell, and that when Dorothy accidentally tosses water on the Witch, the spell is broken. Every year it surprises me—as the Witch is melting, while she still has a voice, it's as if anything can happen. At any moment the monkeys can turn on Dorothy, tear her apart, like they did to the Strawman. Once the Witch is silent, one monkey hobbles over and sniffs the puddle that remains of her—every year I brace myself, in case it turns out different. But every year a guard steps forward and states, simply, *You killed her*, and the spell is broken.

~

Sometimes the story we tell about ourselves can be a type of spell. Sometimes it's about a love that never should have ended,

sometimes it's about a family fortune squandered, and sometimes it's about a war we shouldn't have lost but did. Sometimes
it's an echo of a story from our childhoods, a fairy tale, a story
of what could have been saved, what could have been salvaged,
if we'd just held on a little longer. A story of not giving up, as
they say in A. A., before the miracle comes. Or the story I carry,
unuttered—*If my mother had just made it to Monday, bewildered
but alive.* . . . The structure of these types of stories fit into what
is known as "redemption narratives"—*I once was lost, but now I'm
found.* It's Aristotle's *Poetics*, it's Jesus coming out of the desert,
and now it's reenacted, over and over, on daytime television.
By now it's nearly hardwired into us, but is it possible that this
same narrative structure is now being used, by some, as a justification for the use of torture? The idea being that if we push
the prisoner a little more, if we don't give up when it becomes
unpleasant, if we can ignore the screams, the disfigurement,
the voice in our heads, then the answer will come, the answer
that will save the world. And if the tortured dies in your hands,
without giving the answer, will this mean you were wrong, or
merely that the techniques must be refined? Or if the answer he
gives is worthless, if it is a lie, will that mean we must push a little further, hold on a little longer? Force his head under water?
Make his eyes electric? Does it mean that the doctors must be
brought in, the feeding tubes inserted, the body kept alive? And
if we continue to cling to this way of telling our stories, this
fairy tale, long after we've found our way out of the woods, at
what point can we then be said to be under the effect of some
spell, some enchantment?

the fruit of my deeds

Thich Nhat Hanh gave a dharma talk about a Vietnam vet, an ex-soldier who came to him, unable to sleep. After seeing a buddy killed, this soldier had put rat poison in some sandwiches and left them outside and watched as some children ate them—and since that day what he did has been slowly tearing him apart. *You have only two choices*, Thich Nhat Hanh told the soldier—*continue destroying yourself, or find a way to help five other children. These are your only choices.*

Thich Nhat Hanh always has a contingent of Vietnam vets at his retreats, at least at the ones he holds in America. As the years pass, more and more are from our subsequent wars. I first met some of these vets nearly twenty years ago, and the time I spent with them convinced me to track down Travis, my stepfather, whom I hadn't heard from in years. Travis had served in Vietnam from 1968 to 1970 as a combat Marine—my mother got together with him soon after he got back stateside. They stayed together for four or five tumultuous years, and then they split up.

The years Travis lived with us I never called him my stepfather. He was more of a wild older brother, just a guy who was around for a few years, who taught me how to bang a nail, how to build an addition without pulling a permit, how to "borrow" a stranger's boat to go fishing—then he was gone. When I found him, all those years later, in upstate Vermont, I wanted to ask him two questions: how did he meet my mother, and how did he find out she had died? I'd brought a video camera to film his answers, telling him, telling myself, that I was making a documentary film—the home movie we never had. Later, I would seek out my mother's other boyfriends, ask them the same two questions. What surprised me about Travis was that he felt responsible for her death in some way. He thought she'd used his gun, which I don't even think is true—my mother had her own gun.

~

(1999) Four years after Travis and I reconnected, a filmmaker tracked me down (she'd seen my home movie), and asked if Travis and I would be interested in flying to Vietnam to be part of her documentary film—three combat veterans and three of their children, the vets returning to the scene, their children along to bear witness. The conceit of her film was to examine if war trauma was passed on through generations.

Travis turned fifty on a train from Ho Chi Minh City to Na Trang.

Three weeks into it we spent a day filming a single stretch of road outside Da Nang, where Travis had been stationed. Each night, Travis told us, this dirt road was destroyed by "the gooks," and during the day the Americans would hire the locals to rebuild it. Travis knew, everyone knew, that it was likely that the same ones who destroyed it then rebuilt it the next day. This went on for months. It was, for Travis, as if Sisyphus had to hire someone else to push his rock, thereby denying himself even that pleasure. The day we were filming, Travis spent a long time trying to find the spot he'd spent so many days on thirty years earlier, the exact stretch of road that had been blown up so many times. He spoke with the other vets, pointed to the line of mountains in the distance, tried to line up a photograph of his younger self, standing on that road, with the line of mountains today. While Travis was being interviewed I stood under an umbrella, trying to protect myself from the merciless sun, watching farmers work the rice paddies on either side of the road. Each shoot of rice, once it reached a certain height, had to be transplanted by hand—the bent-over farmers were doing that this day. Travis needed to stand upon the same piece of road he'd stood upon so many years earlier. *Maybe we'd bombed the line of mountain beyond recognition*, José offered—*it happens*. Travis finally had to accept that it wasn't exactly as he remembered. As we drove back to Da Nang we passed small mounds of rice piled along the edge of the road, drying in the sun. Some of the rice got caught up in our tailwind as we passed, rose up in the air, then settled back down to earth.

That night, over dinner, the director announced that the next morning we were to visit the site of the My Lai massacre. It was the first we'd heard of it. The other two vets were not happy about this, and threatened to leave the film if they were forced to go. *No one will be forced to do anything*, the director insisted. The other vets said they'd spent their lives living down My Lai, being called baby-killers by strangers, and this was not why they'd agreed to be part of the film. Travis looked at them. *This is what we all did*, he said. *This is what they meant when they ordered us to clear a village—these guys just got caught*. Travis asked me what I thought. I told him I thought we should go, but that it was up to him.

The next morning the bus pulled up in front of the site of the massacre, which is now a museum, a sacred site. Travis and I walked in together, the camerawoman walking backward in front of us. The other vets and their children remained on the bus. The museum is a small building with framed photographs on the walls, most of the photographs from the *New York Times* or other American newspapers. I remembered seeing a lot of the same photographs when they were first in the *Boston Globe*. At some point Travis told the camerawoman to shut off the camera, that he didn't want to be filmed. Then he walked slowly away from us, talking softly to the translator.

The trip back to Vietnam had been difficult for Travis. He'd only been on an airplane twice in his life—once when he was seventeen and enlisted in the Marines, and again three weeks before this moment. His first days back in-country he couldn't even look a Vietnamese person in the eye, especially anyone in authority, for they all wore the uniforms of the Vietcong. Even the "mama-sans," he couldn't look at them. He told the director a day before we left America that he was planning to bring a small sidearm with him, for "protection." *A gun?* she asked, incredulous. She called me and asked if I thought he was serious. *As far as I know,* I said. She called him back—*Travis, you can't bring a gun with you to Vietnam.*

Fuck it, he said. *I'll buy one over there.*

So Travis and I spent the first few days in Saigon (Ho Chi Minh City) searching the markets for a gun, or even a big knife, but in the end he settled for a bag of marijuana and a massage.

Outside the My Lai museum building is an open field, with small plaques marking the sites of what happened—a spot where some huts stood, a well where a baby was thrown down, the ditch the women and children were herded into. A woman, maybe in her forties, was seated on the grass, her legs folded under her, weeding the lawn very slowly, one stalk at a time. Travis watched her for a while. From a distance I watched Travis watching her. It was as if she was meditating on each blade, considering whether to uproot it (*And now it seems to me the beautiful uncut hair of graves*). I found out later the translator whispered into Travis's ear that the woman had been a child at the time of the massacre, and had survived by hiding beneath the body of her dead mother. Travis nodded, asked if he could speak with her. The translator went to the woman, knelt down, spoke some words, looked back at Travis, gestured for him to come. I watched Travis walk up, say something for the translator to translate. I watched him kneel down before this woman, still seated on the grass, take her hand, kiss it, ask her to forgive him, to forgive America.

istanbul redux

(2007) This is where we pour the words into a jar, as if they were water. As if a jar of water was the same as a river. This is where we try to make a coherent narrative out of chaos. As Amir looks at the photographs of himself, the photographs of what happened three years ago now, he says, *I do not believe it was me that was there.* On the table before him is the wrist tag he was issued, the number he was given, the letters CI after the number, the code which signifies that he was picked up by the CIA. He taps the tiny photograph of himself on the wrist tag— in the photo he has a beard, and his cheeks are gaunt—*Don't you see,* he says, *this man in the photograph, and look at me now.* He smiles. I notice that his arm is trembling slightly by his side.

On our last day in Istanbul, during the last interview, I keep spacing out. Bahir was a soldier in Saddam's army, and he does not smile. His story is less seamless, more fragmented than the others, and I find myself wondering if I believe him. It seems he can't remember much. He looks away as he answers, he starts and stops, he stutters. As I will myself to listen, to pay atten-tion, I realize that it's me—it is the last day and I am so full up with stories of torture and this man before me seems like he hasn't made it out alright. He seems damaged, more damaged than the others, and as I listen, as I pull myself back from wherever it is I go, I realize that his story is one of the hardest. *I was hooded for six months,* Bahir says, *they never took off the hood. And I was shackled to the bars for hours every day. And I was naked, the whole time I was naked. I don't remember anyone's face,* he says, *because I didn't see anyone's face.* Listening to him, I notice that I am sweating, I feel like I will faint. His story often just ends, he cannot continue, he needs a cigarette, he needs to stand and walk around, get some air. We take a break with him, we take many breaks with him. During one break I open the binders of photographs, to a picture of a smiley face magic-markered onto a detainee's nipple. I walk into the hallway and weep.

When we come back from the break the artist asks the translator to tell Bahir how handsome he is, what a pleasure it is to be able to paint him. Bahir listens as this word, "handsome," is translated, smiles slightly—his first smile—then murmurs *Shokran.*

One sometimes needs to be told that one is still beautiful.

~

After everyone leaves Istanbul, I stay on for another week, to visit the Blue Mosque, the Roman aqueducts, a hammam. To write up my notes. In the mosque I read about the use of fetish objects in ancient Islam:

> *Creating a bridge between spiritual and material opposites of daily life, the "Mevlevi" philosophy alters the nature of a simple, ordinary object. A mystical symbol engraved on a "mutekka" (cushion or rest for neck) or a piece of calligraphy*

embroidered on a mailbag gives spirit to the simple material of the object; each item used in daily life evolves into a living being, illuminated by this spirit.

I've come to believe that the function of torture in our society is not about getting information, in spite of what we might want to believe. It is merely about power. It tells the world that there is now no limit to what we will do when we feel threatened. That it is ineffective in gathering information, that it is actually counterproductive in making us any safer, has been clearly documented, it's been known for years. That the box has been opened, and that the use of torture continues, now legally, suggests that it has become, for us, a mystical symbol, no less based on superstition than carving a crescent into a stick. Money, information, these words you are reading—all of this will seem quaint in five hundred years, if we have that long. What they will say when they look back on this time is that torture continued from the death of Christ for over two thousand years—a strange, primitive reenactment. They will see that at first we confused it with passion, which devolved into the Inquisition, and then transformed into what we now call "information." They will see that a handful of maniacs living in caves were able to take down the greatest empire on earth, they will wonder how that could be. All we can tell them is that these maniacs understood our fear, that they transformed into it as we tried to hold on, asking, over and over, our meaningless question.

travis redux

(2007) I spend a day driving route 100 north, the entire length of Vermont, to see Travis—a few years without a face-to-face have slipped past again. I made the trip to ask him about torture, I told myself, but now, sitting across from him, it seems enough to simply catch up. *Sue was with a guy for a while,* Travis tells me—*he'd been in Iraq, came back with a short fuse.* Sue is his daughter. *It must be hard,* I say. *If they were there for a reason it might be different,* Travis mutters. Twelve years ago, when we first reconnected, we'd talked about the first invasion of Iraq, about how he went off the rails—breaking into his estranged wife's apartment, standing at the kitchen stove, burning her clothes item by item on the open flame, until he noticed the blue lights swirling outside. He kicked out a window, crawled on his belly to his truck, outran the cops for a hundred miles. The next morning, once he'd sobered up, a cop knocked on his door—they all knew him—so he turned himself in. The judge went easy, sentenced him to group therapy for vets with post-traumatic stress at the V.A.

A few years later, when we went to Vietnam together, it seemed he'd righted himself—no new stories of run-ins with the law, a jewel-like cabin in the woods he was building for his new girlfriend, his house a little less chaotic. We went to lunch with his kids.

And now, eight years later and three years into another war, I ask him how he's faring. He goes to bed early these days, he tells me, wakes up at three or four, watches the news for an hour or two, then goes to breakfast at Flo's. The other workers—carpenters and plumbers, electricians and mechanics—push some tables together, talk about the war. *Did you know that in Camp Lejune* (a Marine Corps base in North Carolina), *five out of seven wells were contaminated, and the government knew, for five years, and still let the army wives and children drink from them?* I shake my head, but I'm not surprised. The Walter Reed Army Medical Center is in the news these days, paint peeling from the ceilings, roaches in the food, soldiers with head injuries wandering from building to building like an army of zombies, looking for help. We talk about how soup kitchens are set up on bases now, run by church groups, how the rate of suicide among military personnel is the highest it's ever been. Travis is remarkably well informed—*The corporations are getting all the money,* he says, *just like always.* When the war started he went off the rails again, got another DUI, lost his license for eighteen months, got caught driving on a suspended, and ended up spending ten days in lockup, just as the bombs were falling on Baghdad. I bring up Abu Ghraib. *Seems like things got out of control on the night shift,* he says. I tell him about the memos from the White House, about Charles Graner getting high marks for the work he was doing, about how the photos were cropped so that we couldn't see the CIA spooks and the private contractors just outside of the frames. He shakes his head, but it doesn't surprise him. *We look so bad now,* he says. *Invading Iraq was like opening Pandora's box, now no one knows how to stuff everything back in.* We talk about our trip to Vietnam, about My Lai. I tell him that the moment he kissed that survivor's hand and asked her forgiveness was one of the most beautiful things I'd ever witnessed—utterly transformative. I tell him that the same guy who released the My Lai photographs released the Abu Ghraib photographs. Travis shakes his head.

Here for a purpose, he mutters.

Memorabilia from our trip to Vietnam hangs on his walls— a woodblock print of a water buffalo, a straw hat.

Inez is pregnant, I tell him.

Get ready, he smiles.

standard operating procedure

What surprised me the most about meeting the ex-detainees in Istanbul wasn't their descriptions of the torments that had been inflicted on them—after all, I'd seen all the documentaries, read all the transcripts. What surprised me was that before I met them I had somehow created an image in my mind of what an ex-detainee from Abu Ghraib would be like—I pictured someone angry, damaged, maybe tipping toward fundamentalism. And yet each of these men was completely unique, completely human. Each seemed to have taken in what happened in a completely different way, and it still surprises me that this surprised me. What surprises me is that I forgot that each would be fully human, fully complex.

~

(2008) Reading over my notes from those days in Istanbul, I decide not to write what happened, not in detail, the night Amir was dragged on a leash. The information of what happened that night is readily available, and besides, we have the photographs. You might be horrified by the photographs, or you might be deeply saddened. Or you might think that what happened was justified, you might think that it was only a few bad apples, but very few would say that it looked like the MPs were simply trying to help the man on the end of the leash. This is what I imagined, but when I saw Errol Morris's film, and then when I read Philip Gourevitch's companion book—both titled *Standard Operating Procedure*—I was no longer so sure. I paid special attention to the parts which purported to tell the story of what happened the night of Amir on the leash. In the book, in the MP's version, Amir was a wild man—"he kept saying he hated Americans and he wanted us to die." At one point, in their version, Amir is on the floor of an isolation cell, ". . . wounds on his side or his back, and he was laying in feces and urine," and he needs to be moved, but he would not, or could not, budge. Graner claims that he wanted to clean up the cell before the next prisoner arrived. He also claims that he was concerned with how to move Amir without hurting him, so he asked a medic. The medic suggested he place a tie-down strap around Amir's torso, then use it to lift him. But this strap slipped down (up?) around Amir's neck as England held it. Graner thought it looked amusing, so he snapped some pictures. The MPs (and the medic) agree that the photograph looks bad, but they insist that they were merely trying to help Amir (". . . he didn't get hurt . . . ," ". . . my concern was whatever it took to keep him from getting hurt . . ."). Graner and England were with Amir for maybe fifteen minutes that night, they say, just enough time to move him safely.

As I read this account I felt something between amusement and outrage. At first I assumed that Gourevitch was merely giving Graner and England enough rope to hang themselves, as it

were, but this didn't turn out to be the case. In the end, Gourevitch takes the MPs' version of events of that night at their
word, concluding:

> With Gus [Amir] and the tie-down strap . . . when we find out
> the story, the pictures of him with England remain shocking—
> only now the shock lies in the fact that the pictures look worse,
> more deliberately deviant and abusive, than the reality they
> depict.

When we find out the story—despite Gourevitch's claims, and
despite whatever other insights we might glean from his book
(of which there are many), we don't know "the story" of the
night Amir was dragged on that leash from *Standard Operating
Procedure*. What we are offered is merely an endorsement of the
version of the events of that night as told by his torturers. Amir,
the man on the wrong end of the leash, is forced to remain
silent. Amir's version of that night is anything but "anodyne."
As documented by Physicians for Human Rights (PHR), Amir
describes being leashed and dragged, from cell to cell, floor to
floor, for hours. In one cell he is pushed, face-first, Graner's boot
on his head, into that floor soaked with urine and excrement;
in another cell he is sodomized with a broomstick; and in the
final room Graner kicks his testicles, as England steps on his
hand, breaking his finger. At this point Amir passes out and is
dragged back to his cell. Whether you chose to believe Amir
is another issue, but it seems one should at least give as much
ink to him as is given to his tormentors. In Istanbul, as Amir
told us of that night, he held up his broken finger to each of
us, and we each bent in closer to examine it. Nearly four years

later and the damage was no longer visible (*the body hurries to heal itself*) but the doctors have their x-rays, and the Red Cross has their records, and the PHR has corroborated everything. As Amir finished his story that day in Istanbul, he touched the photograph—*This is what happened that night*, he said, *there were other incidences, other nights.*

eclipse

Last night was a lunar eclipse, I held Lulu up to the window to see it. I told her about the sun, about the earth, about the moon, about the eclipse. I said, *You are the sun, I am the moon, I circle around you, and sometimes a shadow falls across your face, sometimes a darkness rises up inside us, but it isn't real, we cannot believe it is real.* I held her head like a sun, and we moved around the room, singing, *Little darlin, it's been a long cold lonely winter,* until she stopped crying and fell asleep.

Before she came, if I tried to *vis-u-al-ize* her, I'd always end up back on that rollercoaster, in a broken-down car climbing a rickety hill, this tiny baby at the apex. As I'd reach her, as I'd take her in my arms, the car would begin its inevitable descent, then drop into freefall. Part of my fear, if unarticulated, was that as we fell I wouldn't be able to hold on to her, that she would fly out of my grip—I couldn't imagine that she could simply fall with me, safe in my arms.

fourteen

wrong ocean

(2008) I wake up early, carry Lulu from the bed to the living room, let Inez sleep in. Lulu smiles at the daylight, at the shadows crossing the brick wall outside the kitchen window. She seems happy that the sun came back. It's so simple. At dusk she looks in terror out the windows, seemingly confused by the darkness, by where everything goes. In this she is like me—I smile in the morning, and as the day progresses I get more and more confused, by everything coming at me. *Overstimulated*, they call us. *Sundowners*. At sundown she cries, simple as that. *Nothing you can do that isn't done*, I sing to her, swaying slowly around the kitchen with her in my arms—*nothing you can sing that isn't sung*.

~

The book I read after my mother died, the how-to-deal-with-trauma book, had failed to say when change could resume, when one could go on. So, year after year, I lived on the boat. Year after year I rowed my body out, scanned the shoreline, waited. Ten years—why did it take so long to get my feet back on the ground, why did it take so long to lose my sea legs? The boat was built the same year my mother was born (1939, the same year *The Wizard of Oz* was released, the same year Freud died), and therefore contained something of her, or so it seemed. We'd scattered her ashes in the Atlantic—living on the boat was as close to her as I could get. You could say I felt held by the water, you could say I was, like Dorothy, only trying to find my way back home. It worked, for a while, to dissolve into something larger than myself, until by the end not even the ocean was big enough to contain it.

giddy-up

(2008) My grandfather, my mother's father, calls in the Irish
girl who takes care of him by ringing a small brass bell, which
is shaped like a crane. I am visiting him a few weeks before
Lulu is born. He holds the bell by its beak as he shakes it. If I
let myself imagine what I would like to have to remember him
by, all I can imagine is this bell, this crane. Framed on the wall
behind his head is a silhouette, I remember my mother making it during a blackout, my brother aiming a flashlight at my
head, my mother tracing my profile with a pencil onto the black
paper tacked to the wall. I remember her taking it down, then
cutting it out. The Irish girl comes in, smiles, leans over the
bed, asks, *And what can I do for you now,* her blond pigtails nearly
brushing his face, but already he has closed his eyes again. As
a girl my mother wore her hair in pigtails, I have pictures, I've
seen the painting of her beside the horse. I even remember her
in pigtails, sometimes, when she was my mother. Strange, but
in my grandfather's room, in his whole house, there are no photographs of her. It's not that it's a house without photographs—
walls, bookcases, tabletops, all sit thick with cousins, uncles,
strangers—photographs are everywhere. But none of my
mother, and as for my brother and I, only this one silhouette—
it's as if our branch had been erased, and was now merely a

shadow. Grandpa and I never talk about my mother, not really, but I interviewed him once about her, when I made the documentary, the home movie, about her ex-boyfriends. I wanted to ask him one of the questions I'd asked each of them—*How did you find out she'd died?* Grandpa wore a suit for the interview, sat upright behind his desk, but seconds into it he began crying—I'd never seen him cry before. *I didn't know how to help her,* he said. Ten years later, ten more years of not uttering her name, and I've been sitting with him when I can, since he broke his hip. Sometimes he talks to me about the universe, sometimes about his fever dreams, and sometimes I transcribe what he says in a small notebook. Both of us know that this bed is his deathbed—he will die two days after Lulu's born, he will never hold her. The Irish girl and I are with him now. He opens his eyes, tells us his dream—*I was walking down a mountain road, and a man approached me in a carriage, drawn by four horses. The carriage stopped beside me, opened the door, but I said I'd rather walk.* He smiles, then he closes his eyes. The Irish girl winks at me, leans over him, asks again what she can do for him. He opens his eyes, takes a pigtail in each of his hands—*Giddy-up,* he says.

don't be cruel

(2008) Elvis (*The King*) showed up on a hotel television recently, as I tried to channel surf my way into sleep. I was in California for two days, away from Inez and Lulu for the first time. In the film (*Roustabout? Spinout?*) Elvis played a musician needing to talk to the taxman—in terms of plot, that's as far as I got. I couldn't take my eyes off him—oozing this big, dumb animal magnetism, he seemed to embody America.

Plato (more generously than I) put it this way:

> Any one who has common sense will remember that the bewilderments of the eyes are of two kinds, and arise from two causes, either from coming out of the light or from going into the light . . . and he who remembers this when he sees any one whose vision is perplexed and weak, will not be too ready to laugh; he will first ask whether that soul of man has come out of the brighter life, and is unable to see because unaccustomed to the dark, or having turned from darkness to the day is dazzled by excess of light.

By the time Elvis made this film he was perhaps already well on his way to bewildering himself through drugs, or perhaps he could simply sense the bewilderment to come—stranded on his la-z-boy, his silver chalice of pills, his fried peanut-butter sandwiches. As I watched him on screen I wondered if the drugs were already seeping into every pore. Sometimes all we have is our shadows, sometimes whole years of our lives can pass, mere shadow talking to shadow.

~

(2004) During the televised presidential debates, a few months after the release of the Abu Ghraib photographs, we got a glimpse of our president's shadow, when he referred to his daughters, who had recently spent a night or two in the drunk tank, as he had when he was their age (and, in the spirit of full [*full?*] disclosure, as I had as well):

LEHRER: Ninety second response, Senator.

KERRY: Well, first of all, I appreciate enormously the personal comments the president just made. And I share them with him. I think only if you're doing this—and he's done it more than I have in terms of the presidency—can you begin to get a sense of what it means to your families. And it's tough. And so I acknowledge that his daughters—I've watched them. I've chuckled a few times at some of their comments.

(LAUGHTER)

And . . .

BUSH: I'm trying to put a leash on them.

(LAUGHTER)

KERRY: Well, I know. I've learned not to do that.

(LAUGHTER)

I'm trying to put a leash on them. This, as you remember, was only a few months after the Abu Ghraib photos were made public, several of which showed Lynndie England dragging (albeit half-heartedly) a naked Iraqi (Amir) by the neck on a leash. It is the only vague, indirect mention of torture in the entire debates, when many were still trying to find a way to put these shadows back into their boxes.

~

(2006) Bush is discussing the Supreme Court ruling in the Hamdan case with reporters. *Please,* Bush jokes, *remember that Elvis classic when you ask me your questions—Don't Be Cruel.* Bush is standing beside Prime Minister Koizumi of Japan (Koizumi is, apparently, an Elvis freak). Each man smiles into the cameras. They have just come from Graceland. *Don't be cruel,* Bush jokes, and the reporters, his parrots, laugh, and then they ask their empty questions, and Bush, essentially, answers nothing—his shadow has already spoken. *Don't be cruel,* Elvis sings, and now his shadow keeps singing, but it isn't a plea not to be cruel to everyone, it never was. *Don't be cruel,* Elvis pleads, *to a heart that's true.* Elvis sings, Bush sings, his parrots sing, Koizumi sings, and now I find myself singing along as well, a song so deep, yet uninvited, in my head.

~

(2008) Two days ago the president announced, through a spokesman, and without apparent shame, that we have tortured in the past and we will torture again. When it is revealed that his top aides met to discuss specific torture techniques, Bush will claim, petulantly, to have been in on the discussions as well. Endgame—no more smoke and mirrors, no more claiming state's secrets, it's cards-on-the-table time. Nearly four years since the photographs were released—*This is who we are now*, the president seems to say, *this is who we've always been*. Once there was plausible deniability, but really they—we—haven't tried to deny anything, not very much. We all know what was done, we always knew, and now (*the word made flesh*) it has merely been uttered.

solaris (house of strange fathers)

In Andrei Tarkovsky's 1972 film *Solaris*, an astronaut wakes up on his first morning on a spaceship, his wife asleep beside him, her arm over his chest. The only problem is that his wife had committed suicide some years earlier, so this woman, it seems, is a product of his imagination, or of his neurosis—the physical form of his desire, or of his guilt. The spaceship, to use Zizek's phrase, has become an "id machine." As Zizek says: *It's relatively easy to get rid of a real person. You can abandon him or her, kill him or her, whatever. But a ghost is much harder to get rid of. It sticks to you as a sort of spectral presence.* Another astronaut, as the dead woman picks herself up from the floor of the spaceship for the umpteenth time, simply shrugs—*It's horrifying, isn't it. I'll never get used to these constant resurrections.*

~

A year after Lulu is born I learn that "Abu Ghraib" translates in Arabic to *House of Strange Fathers*—maybe this is the key, maybe it's as simple as that, the reason I've felt compelled to wrestle these shadows. My mother's father was dying, I was shepherding my father closer to his last breath (or at least out of his apartment), and I was on the threshold of becoming a father myself.

My parents' lives have always acted as a map, but it's been so hard to follow sometimes—much of it seemed to simply mark out places I should avoid. Yet these were the places I always found myself in—where else would I go?

~

Last night I got a call from Eli, a friend I spent many days and many nights with when I was living in Rome. Eli had set me up with my apartment when I first landed. Eli's father died a year ago. I ask him how he's faring, and he tells me that it feels strange to admit, but he actually feels more grounded now that his father is gone. *Grounded*—it's the same word I've been using when I try to articulate the changes that Lulu has brought into my life—*grounded*. Buying a house didn't do it, writing a book didn't. Maybe "grounded" simply means an awareness of being one step closer to being put into the ground, maybe that's why I've resisted it all these years. Or maybe it was just my nature, to live on the water, to wander. Now, watching Lulu lift herself off the floor, it all feels right, to have my legs under me, for once.

~

The calendar by the register in the café where I go to write is from *The Far Side*. The page for today is this: Two prison guards lead a clown down a hallway to the electric chair. One says to the other, *I don't think I'll be able to tell my kids about this one.* This year the Nobel in physics went to three Japanese astrophysicists who, as I understand it, proved that the universe only exists because of a mistake—if the laws of the universe were in per-fect harmony, nothing would have come into being. The Big Bang wouldn't have happened, because everything would have been fine as it was. *This proves there's no perfect theory of the universe*, the radio commentator tells us.

here comes the sun

Every Christmas, for a few years, which seemed and still seems forever, the new Beatles album waited beneath the tree. Some years there were even two—1968, the Year of the Monkey—two perfect squares wrapped in red and green tissue paper. We already half-knew most of the songs, but we didn't know all the words. One opened up like a kid's picture book: John Paul Ringo and George looking out at us in the uniforms of some psychedelic army; John Paul Ringo and George walking across a street in white suits and black suits and barefoot and in jeans. Before that day we'd had to sit in the car and wait for "Here Comes the Sun" or "Hey Jude" to end—no one, until that moment, had ever heard "Hey Jude," but from that moment on it would always be there, from then on it would never not be there.

A few years after the Beatles broke up, I had a paper route, delivering the *Boston Globe* before the sun came up. Sometimes my mother would drive me, if it had snowed in the night, if I was late for school, her car warm and waiting after I trudged back between houses, the radio playing low. Most mornings I was alone, on my bike or walking, and I would pause under a certain streetlight to see what was happening in the world. I would follow a story for the days or weeks it would appear, first as a headline, then as it moved further and further into the body of the paper. Vietnam. Watergate. Patty Hearst. One morning the photograph on the front page was of a plane that had crashed at Logan Airport, thirty miles to the north. The plane had tried to take off but something had kept it on the ground—maybe there was ice on the wings, maybe one of the wings was broken, maybe a screw was loose. Or maybe it had crashed trying to land, maybe it overshot the runway, maybe it's brakes failed— I can't remember now. All I know for certain is that everyone died—everyone, that is, except one man, and this one man, this survivor, was the reason I read the paper everyday, searching for news of him. Let's call him Manuel. He stayed alive for days, which became weeks, horribly burnt, wrapped in gauze, immobilized, but alive. I searched the paper every day for word of him, every day my mother would ask me if there was anything in the paper about him. I wanted him to pull through, for some reason I was desperate for one person to walk away from this impossible disaster.

fifteen

pond

(*2008*) Hungry, Lulu cries her small cry with the first light (*cell by cell the baby made herself*). A few minutes before this she'd let out a coo (*the cells made cells*), a coo which became the texture of the dream I was having (*that is to say the baby is made largely of milk*), a coo which meant that everything was going to be alright. I get out of bed, step into the cold of the barn, and make my way over to her room, which we insulated and now heat with an oil-filled electric radiator, like our room will be, one day, once—if—we get around to hanging the doors. The rest of the barn, which I pass through quickly, is essentially the same weather as the outside world, and this morning the outside world is cool, and thick with fog. Since living in the barn, there have been nights where I've woken up to take a piss and been stopped on the way to the toilet, the dark air around me filled with fireflies. Or if there was lightning outside, then inside the barn would brighten with lightning as well. But those were summer nights, when we'd sleep with the big sliding doors left open.

After I change Lulu and feed her we play together quietly for a while on the carpet—our favorite game, right now, is *daddy's gonna get you*. Then we make our way down to the pond, let Inez sleep in a little longer, Lulu's little body strapped to my chest like a parachute.

We'd moved into the barn last May so that we could rent out the house. Money got tight after the baby came, so in the spring I'd offered to fix the barn up, since I knew how to do it, or at least I knew enough friends I could call on to help. For years, before I even met Inez, the barn had become a place to gather junk: a lawn mower that doesn't start; a hundred mismatched windows; another entire barn, dismantled and neatly stacked; a padlocked refrigerator.

The barn is a hundred and fifty years old, held together by huge sixty-foot-long hickory beams, a quality of tree that hasn't grown here, maybe anywhere, for nearly a hundred years now. The roof is slate, kestrels (windhovers) live in the cupola—anything could happen in that barn. It could be a theater, it could hold an airplane. You could build a room inside it, a hidey-hole for when things got bad. By the time Lulu and I make it to the pond my boots are wet with dew. Steam is rising from the water, the surface utterly still.

Until a month or so ago, the land had become so overgrown that you could only glimpse the pond as you walked along the narrow path connecting one meadow to the next. At night you could hear the bullfrogs, but at night it's hard to locate where sound is coming from. It seemed to come from the low point in the land, the place a pond would be, if there was a pond. I asked Inez about it, but all she'd heard was in the winter one couldn't skate on it because it was so deep it wouldn't freeze, and in the summer you couldn't swim in it because it wasn't big enough. This seemed contradictory, but not being able to see it clearly, I couldn't verify either claim. Every year the wild roses had grown thicker, sending out their long tendrils of thorns, which tore at your arms if you tried to pull them back to see a little more. From what I could glimpse it was possible that the pond was no bigger than a bucket, which would mean it wasn't a pond at all. In all likelihood it was simply vernal, evaporating in the summer, leaving only a muddy patch. In the summer, when the undergrowth was thickest, this seemed completely possible.

Shortly after we moved into the barn I decided to try to clear it.

The land hadn't been brush-hogged for eight years or so, which is why the wild roses and the locusts and the sycamore had taken over. I found someone who had the machine that could do the job. By the end of the first day he'd gouged a path to the pond's edge, and I was able to walk up to it and look across to the other side. Hundreds of frogs splashed the surface as I approached, the water tea-colored, a few trees draped their branches into it, their leaves floating on the surface. The pond wasn't large—one could swim the length of it in about ten strokes, I estimated, once a little more was cleared away.

I would spend the next several weeks, whenever I had a free hour or so, usually when Lulu was napping, clearing away the pond's mucky edge, which the brush hog hadn't been able to reach. It was now August, and a friend was renting the house. Later he'd tell me that he'd look out at me, hacking away at the undergrowth, and wonder if working on the book about Lulu and torture hadn't driven me a little mad. From his window the pond was still invisible. All he could see was that after an hour or so I would come back up the hill, shirtless, sweat dripping off my nose, my legs muddy, my arms bleeding from the thorns. At night we'd have dinner and I'd talk about the pond, how beautiful it was, how lately, at dawn, Lulu and I had been seeing a heron, or perhaps it was a bittern, sitting on a branch, watching over the water. I didn't know if the heron had always been there, no one knew, because until that moment no one had even seen the pond, not for many years. In the weeks I worked on clearing it I didn't write a word, and it is very possible that I didn't have a thought in my head, beyond the thought of Lulu (my Fairy Queen), and that pond.

the lord god bird

(2004) In February a birdwatcher in Arkansas claims to have
seen an ivory-billed woodpecker, also known as the Lord God
Bird, a species listed as extinct for sixty years now. If true this
would be a very good thing—it would be as if a lover you
thought long dead rang your doorbell. Then, at the end of April,
around the same time the Abu Ghraib photographs appear,
another Arkansas man claims that he has made a four-second
video of an ivory-billed woodpecker in flight. Ornithologists
weep *(If you don't weep now, when will you weep?)*. One says, *It
shows there's hope, against all odds*. But shortly thereafter an albino
dolphin, a species unique to the Yangtze, known to the locals as
the spirit of the river, washes up on shore, and it is feared to be
the last. And then the honeybees begin to leave their hives, as
if they have forgetten their way home, as if they are lost. "Hive
Collapse Syndrome," the beekeepers dub it, and offer several
possible reasons. One is that the electromagnetic waves from
cellphone towers are confusing them. Another is the effects of
a super pesticide, a nicotine derivative, which doesn't merely sit
on the leaves, but actually becomes part of the plant, causing
the predatory insects (and humans as well, presumably) who
eat them to lose their memory, act erratically, and die.

~

(2009) My father now has a bed by a window, now his clothes are always clean, now he eats three meals a day. He's living in a "long-term care facility," a nursing home. He is still on a little Ativan, which seems to dissolve his anxiety. The doors to the outside are kept locked, so he can't wander off and get any liquor. This is the first time I have ever known him to be sober—his stories are different, he no longer tells the same handful, over and over. But his mind is shot. He knows who I am, dimly, but he cannot remember when he last saw me, or anything about my life. I could tell him a hundred times that he is now a grandfather, and it simply will not sink in. The last time we visited we brought Lulu, so they could meet. Maybe then she would become real to him. We even took a photograph of him holding her, and, at least for that one moment, they both look joyful. But as the hour progressed, my father had a hard time keeping it all in his head. Was Lulu his daughter or his granddaughter? Was Inez his sister or his wife? At one point he takes me aside. *I have to talk to you*, he says—*they're treating me like I'm a millionaire, and I got no money. I don't know what I'll do when they find out*. I pass a few folded dollar bills into his hand. *I'm working on it*, I assure him.

~

At the end of *They Came Back*, the French zombie film, one woman nearly follows her lover back into the earth. It's always a choice, the film suggests. Fuck zombies, I mutter to myself, fuck ghosts—only those who have never lost anyone believe in the undead. Fuck resurrections, fuck transmogrification, the only miracle is flesh and consciousness, the only miracle is now. Lulu is the only miracle (the word "Lulu" is the only miracle). That Inez and I keep figuring it out—to be together, to be with Lulu, that it's all a daily practice—this is the only miracle. It's so simple—sometimes we just need to be held, sometimes we just need to be told we're beautiful. Sometimes we might even need to believe that the dead will come back, but they never come back, not really. It's just a dream, maybe the same dream that makes you feel safe as you try to force an answer from someone tied to a chair. We lived for so long believing the ivory-billed woodpecker was gone, but it wasn't gone. It had merely flown deeper into the woods, and then it flew back. The only question now is how long it will stay.

~

(2008) At dawn I sit on the couch and slide *The Wizard of Oz* into my computer, Lulu asleep in my arms. Almost immediately, for some reason, tears well up in my eyes. Dorothy, right from the start, is trying to get back home—mythic, yet simple as a fairy tale, like following a trail of breadcrumbs through a dark forest. Lulu stirs, smiles up at me, reaches for my nose, then gets distracted by the leafy plant behind my head. I shut the computer, a pure simple joy filling the room. The leaves she is staring at now, she can't even see them, not the green, not the shapes, she is simply staring into this world—everything hazy, but slowly coming into focus. Soon she will have her Wizard of Oz moment, the rods and cones in her eyes already developing, soon the world will transform from black and white to color, like the moment Dorothy first steps into Oz.

[some notes]

Listed below, by chapter, are the principal works referred to in the text, as well as other works that supplied me with facts or influenced my thinking. Also, if it seemed more needed to be said on a topic, those thoughts are included below as *notes*. Most of the articles mentioned below can be linked to through www .nickflynn.org.

a field guide to getting lost

Rebecca Solnit, *A Field Guide to Getting Lost* (Viking, 2005), p. 22.

Erik Jonsson, *Inner Navigation: Why We Get Lost and How We Find Our Way* (Scribner, 2002).

handshake

Sam Harris, *The End of Faith* (Norton, 2004), pp. 199, 193, 52.

crank

note: That the PEN judges were three women somehow bewilders me, in much the same way that some of the torturers at Abu Ghraib are women bewilders me—is this what the pioneers of feminism envisioned? Angela Davis points out that by now the term *equal opportunity* has been twisted to often simply mean *equal access to the instruments of oppression.*

note: The reviews of *The End of Faith* cited are from the *Chicago Tribune* (no mention of torture), the *San Francisco Chronicle* (no mention of torture), and the *New York Sun* (no mention of torture).

note: For more on the secret history of America's involvement in torture, see School of the Americas Watch (www.soaw.org).

pleaid

Edgar Allan Poe, *The Pit and the Pendulum: It was not that I feared to look upon things horrible, but that I grew aghast lest there should be nothing to see.*

welcome to the year of the monkey

Seymour M. Hersh, *Chain of Command* (HarperCollins, 2004).

note: For one (of many) ongoing, grassroots rebuilding efforts in New Orleans, see www.paydirt.org (Mel Chin).

one simple question

note: The observation about schools named after Martin Luther King comes from Jonathan Kozol, *Shame of a Nation.* For good work being done in Harlem schools, see Geoffrey Canada's Harlem Children's Zone (www.hcz.org).

note: The third and final stanza of Stafford's *A Story That Could Be True* is:

They miss the whisper that runs
any day in your mind,
"Who are you really, wanderer?"—
and the answer you have to give
no matter how dark and cold
the world around you is:
"Maybe I'm a king."

you don't take pictures
note: Torture apologists cited in this chapter include Rush Limbaugh, Trent Lott, and Charles Krauthammer (*Weekly Standard*, 2 December 2005).

note: The secretary of defense at that time was Donald Rumsfeld. Rumsfeld grew up in the same town as a close friend of mine, where, as a child, he was known around the neighborhood as "Bully Don," the meanest kid on the playground.

note: . . . *was it possible they were there and not haunted?*—Michael Herr, *Dispatches* (approximately).

thrown it all away
note: "Since You're Gone" is from the third Cars album, *Shake It Up*, which didn't come out until 1981, but by then we were driving smaller cars and listening to cassettes.

the book of daniel
Dante, *Inferno* (my own translation).

god's loneliness (known)

note: The repeated refrain of *God's loneliness . . .* is from Fanny Howe's essay "Bewilderment," in her collection *The Wedding Dress: Meditations on Word and Life* (University of California Press, 2003).

the allegory of the cave

note: "Jewish lightning" was my mother's phrase for when someone burns down his or her own house to collect the insurance money, which, like the phrase my grandmother used for Brazil nuts ("nigger toes"), did to me what such derogatory expressions tend to do to children—they confused the hell out of me, and left me with a deep sadness. *Do not water the seeds of hatred,* Thich Nhat Hanh urges.

note: Some scholars dispute whether Plato dreamed this allegory, or whether it came to him when fully awake.

note: In 2005, in a debate in Chicago, John Yoo, a former Department of Justice lawyer and one of the architects of Bush's torture doctrine, stated that, in his opinion, the president has the authority to order a child's testicles crushed, if deemed in the interests of the United States. Yoo now teaches law at the University of California, Berkeley.

note: Elaine Pagels, in *The Origin of Satan*, argues that Satan in the Old Testament was more obstructionist, rather than an active force of evil.

note: The vice president, Dick Cheney, was speaking on *Meet the Press*, 16 September 2001.

note: The clandestine program known as "extraordinary rendition" was begun by the Clinton administration, and then expanded geometrically under G. W. Bush. In August 2009, the Obama administration announced it would continue the program.

note: The secretary of state at that time was Colin Powell. In his autobiography, *My American Journey*, Powell discusses, with some pride, the effectiveness of a program used during Vietnam, whereby military-aged men (MAM) would be targeted for execution, even if they were unarmed—*If a helo spotted a peasant in black pajamas who looked remotely suspicious, a possible MAM, the pilot would circle and fire in front of him. If he moved, his movement was judged evidence of hostile intent, and the next burst was not in front, but at him.* Targeting unarmed civilians for execution is deemed a war crime by most of the world.

note: An essay on the ineffectiveness and degradation of torture by a former Soviet human rights activist, Vladimir Bukovsky (*Washington Post,* 18 December 2005), begins with an old Soviet joke from the 1950s: *One nasty morning Comrade Stalin discovered that his favorite pipe was missing. Naturally, he called in his henchman, Lavrenti Beria, and instructed him to find the pipe. A few hours later, Stalin found it in his desk and called off the search. "But, Comrade Stalin," stammered Beria, "five suspects have already confessed to stealing it."*

john doe

note: Touch any strand and the whole web trembles—Stanley Kunitz.

note: Coincidence is just the tip of the iceberg—Tad Flynn.

horror vacui

note: Did I leave out the part where John Doe died on me, or am I simply fated (samsara) to keep confessing to this one night?

proteus (sciamachy)

Saadi Youssef, from his poem "America, America" (last stanza), collected in *Without an Alphabet, Without a Face: Selected Poems*, translated by Khaled Mattawa (Graywolf Press, 2002).

Fanny Howe, from her essay *Bewilderment*, collected in *The Wedding Dress: Meditations on Word and Life* (University of California Press, 2003).

istanbul

note: The lawyer is Susan Burke, of the law firm Burke O'Neil LLC. The companies named in the lawsuit are Titan and Caci—cases are also pending against Jeppesen/Boeing (see Trevor Paglen, *Torture Taxi* [Melville House, 2006], or Stephen Grey, *Ghost Plane* [St. Martin's, 2007]) as well as against Blackwater, the mercenary-for-hire corporation (see Jeremy Scahill, *Blackwater* [Nation Books, 2007]). Daniel Heyman, Tara McKelvey, Chris Bartlett, and Jennifer Schelter are some of the artists who have participated in the gathering of testimonies with Burke's legal team.

istanbul (dream, reality)
note: Daniel Heyman also etched portraits and text onto copper plates—he had to etch each word backwards, and each sentence right to left, which, oddly, beautifully, mirrored Arabic script.

transmogrification
Backbeat (film), 1994.

istanbul (the happy-bus)
note: Physicians for Human Rights (PHR) examined "Amir"—his story is documented in *Broken Laws, Broken Lives—Medical Evidence of Torture by U.S. Personnel and Its Impact,* 2008.

two dogs
note: The idea that two dogs live inside us is a Native American parable—George Bernard Shaw is often credited with first bringing it to Western audiences.

facts about water
note: Elsewhere I've written that the last words in my mother's suicide note were *Why don't you use the gun?*—which is true, yet these words seemed to have been dictated by a voice in her head which was not her own.

the tricky part
Martin Moran, *The Tricky Part* (Beacon Press, 2005).

mistress yin
Stephen Elliott, *My Girlfriend Comes to the City and Beats Me Up* (Cleis Press, 2006).

the invisible city
note: He already had the water . . . —Thich Nhat Hanh, on the Buddha.

unknown, known
note: Here, Bullet is the title of a book of poems by Brian Turner, a veteran of the Iraq War (Operation Iraqi Freedom).

note: The one book of poetry in our house when I was growing up was *Ariel*—it had a sacred place on my mother's bedside table. Janet Malcolm, in *The Silent Woman: Sylvia Plath & Ted Hughes* (Knopf, 1994), writes:

> Life, of course, never gets anyone's entire attention. Death always remains interesting, pulls us, draws us. As sleep is necessary to our physiology, so depression seems necessary to our psychic economy. In some secret way, Thanatos nourishes Eros as well as opposes it. The two principles work in covert concert: though in most of us Eros dominates, in none of us is Thanatos completely subdued. However—and this is the paradox of suicide—to *take* one's life is to behave in a more active, assertive, "erotic" way than to helplessly watch as one's life is *taken away* from one by inevitable mortality. Suicide thus engages both the death-hating and the death-loving parts of us: on some level, perhaps we may envy the suicide even as we pity him. (p. 58)

sheepfucker
Naomi Klein, *The Shock Doctrine: The Rise of Disaster Capitalism* (Metropolitan Books, 2007).

note: My statement to Harris that his book contains *much to admire* is specious hyperbole. In *The End of Faith*, Harris rails against religious fundamentalism, which seems obvious, as well as against religious moderates, which seems intolerant.

note: As early as 2004, several former U.S. military interrogators, including Anthony Lagoranis, Eric Fair, and Sam Provance, each of whom had served in Iraq, came out publicly against torture. In 2007, a group of World War II veterans, who had interrogated Nazis at Fort Hunt (N.Y.), also expressed their outrage at the use of torture, which they deem both ineffective and immoral (*Washington Post*, "Fort Hunt's Quiet Men Break Silence on WWII," 6 October 2007). These individuals were followed by thirty retired admirals and generals who, in a joint statement, published in the *New York Times*, also called for an end to torture (12 December 2007). By 2008, "Two hundred leaders ranging form former secretaries of state and counter-terrorism experts to religious leaders and legal experts issued a call today for a presidential executive order that would ban torture and cruel treatment of detainees" (*Nukes & Spooks*, 25 June 2008).

note: Fred Marchant, in his introduction to *Another World Instead: The Early Poems of William Stafford, 1937–1947* (Graywolf Press, 2008) writes:

In "The Iliad, or the Poem of Force," an essay written during the first year of World War II, [Simone] Weil celebrates the virtues of hesitation, pausing, swerving. Examining several blood-stained scenes in the poem, she notes that those who conquer and kill—be they Greek or Trojan—are inexorable. No one imposes the slightest halt in what they are doing. No one, she writes, insists on "that interval of hesitation, wherein lies all our consideration for our brothers in humanity."

It is also important to note that many of the Greek playwrights— Sophocles, Euripides, etc.—came from the military, and wrote their plays as a way to deal with the trauma they'd witnessed, both in battle and in the returning warriors (what we now call post-traumatic stress disorder).

the ticking is the bomb
note: The story of the man crying *Allah* every time he is struck by his U.S. captors is from Alex Gibney's documentary film *Taxi to the Dark Side.*

note: In a critique of the television drama *24*, Slovoj Zikek writes:

There was a further "ethical problem" for Himmler: how to make sure the executioners, while perform- ing these terrible tasks, remained human and dignified. His answer was Krishna's message to Arjuna in the Bhagavad-Gita (Himmler always had in his pocket a leather-bound edition): *act with inner distance; do not get*

fully involved ("The Depraved Heroes of *24* are the Himm-
lers of Hollywood," *The Guardian*, 10 January 2006).

the fallen tower
note: Many of the frescoes in Assisi's upper basilica are Giotto's,
but the fresco of the fallen tower is in the lower basilica—I am
uncertain whether it is, in fact, a Giotto.

note: The trend of using torture to sell things began immediately
after the release of the Abu Ghraib photographs, for everything
from Diesel jeans (images of flagellation) to Charles Schwab
(*Nickel and dimed? Try quartered!*) to Altoids (*Ve have vays of making
you talk*).

paradise lost
John Milton, *Paradise Lost.*

note: Herman Melville commented on *Paradise Lost*: *Milton's
Satan is morally very superior to his God, as whoever perseveres despite
adversity and torture is superior to whoever, in cold Vengeance, takes
the most horrible revenge on his enemies.*

mexico (the war)
note: One of Duras's biographers is fairly certainly that her depiction of herself as a torturer is likely hubris, overcompensating for
the fact that she actually worked for Nazi censors during the war
(*New York Review of Books*, June 2008).

note: In fact, a universal ban on torture was implemented by
most Western countries centuries before the Geneva Conven-

tions. George Washington put it this way: "Should any American solider be so base and infamous as to injure any [prisoner] . . . I do most earnestly enjoin you to bring him to such severe and exemplary punishment as the enormity of the crime may require. Should it extend to death itself, it will not be disproportional to its guilt at such a time and in such a cause . . . for by such conduct they bring shame, disgrace and ruin to themselves and their country."

dear reader (oblivion)
Margaret Wise Brown, *Goodnight Moon* (Harper, 1947).

roulette
note: Freud came to believe that the death drive (*thanatos*), represents an urge, inherent in all living things, to return to an original state of calm: in other words, an inorganic or dead state. "An original state of calm," though, sounds like it could also be a meditative state.

too loud a solitude
note: In Bohumil Hrabal's novel, *Too Loud a Solitude* (Harcourt, 1990), the hero is, among other things, a hoarder. The form this hoarding takes is that he collects books from his job at the dump, so many that by the time we meet him hundreds of volumes strain the rickety shelf over his bed, threatening to one day collapse and crush him in his sleep. At night he lies in bed, reading, occasionally glancing up, thinking about this, imagining this collapse. As I remember it he is finally crushed beneath his salvaged books, but I could be misremembering.

note: Unlike my father, who'd be insane not to drink, I become insane when I do.

lexington, kentucky
Alfred McCoy, *A Question of Torture* (Metropolitan Books, 2006).

the gulag archipelago
Aleksandr Solzhenitsyn, *The Gulag Archipelago* (Harper & Row, 1973), pp. 103, 177.

note: The Button Man, my father's book, will likely remain forever unpublished. Solzhenitsyn, as far as I know, died unaware of either my father or his writings.

note: By 1963 the CIA had created its own torture manual, titled KUBARK. In 2002, the training program to prepare soldiers in the event of capture and torture, known as SERE (for Survival, Evasion, Resistance, Escape), was "reverse-engineered" by two APA psychologists (James Mitchell and Bruce Jessen) and subsequently used on prisoners at Guantánamo, Abu Ghraib, and in CIA "black sites." The SERE program was based on Chinese Communist techniques used during the Korean War to obtain confessions, many of them intentionally false, from American prisoners—think *The Manchurian Candidate* crossed with *The Banality of Evil.* Think also of Ibn al-Shaykh al-Libi (mentioned earlier), whose false confession led to the justification of the invasion of Iraq. (See also Mark Danner, "The Red Cross Torture Report: What It Means," *New York Review of Books,* 30 April 2009).

my augean stables

Daniel Johnston, "Like a Monkey in a Zoo" from the album *Songs of Pain*, 1981.

Solzhenitsyn, *The Gulag Archipelago*, p. 275.

two strong men

question: Would Russian hipsters drink at a bar called CIA?

lisbon

note: As Portugal had no standing military at that time, I wondered who paid these soldiers. Two years later, during the Iran-Contra hearings, Portugal was identified as "Country B," the conduit for arms to Iran—the soldier I encountered was, quite possibly, part of a paramilitary unit funded by the United States (in other words, funded by me). This is, perhaps, as close as I've come to S&M, that is, paying someone to punch me. Or maybe it is merely another instance of *sciamachy*, wrestling with one's own shadow. I encountered the same type of nonregulation soldiers running around Costa Rica during the Contra War, and in fact nearly got punched again for taking a picture of one of them.

heroic uses of concrete

Webster's New Twentieth Century Dictionary of the English Language.

the navigator

note: Keaton's character, of course, is not alone on the ship—his love interest also stowed aboard, but it takes awhile for them to meet up.

piero della francesca

note: In a related story, by 2008 we in the U.S. once again broke our own record for the number of our fellow citizens behind bars—more than one in one hundred adults are in jail or prison (if you are black the percentage is one in nine). This is a higher percentage of the population than in any other country in the world.

note: The ACLU obtained documents through the Freedom of Information Act which cite that 90 percent of the detainees at Abu Ghraib were known to be innocent.

note: The phrase *Son of God* had many meanings in Jesus' time, one of which was "a son born without a father," which, by all accounts, Jesus was. Just as the phrase *virgin birth* could mean simply an unmarried woman giving birth, which, by all accounts, describes Jesus' mother (see Geza Vermes, *The Authentic Gospel of Jesus* [Penguin, 2005]).

the passion (misnamed)

note: In this (mis)reading, rather than a run-of-the-mill state-sponsored execution, the Crucifixion becomes Jesus' (or God's) choice, a sacred sacrifice for the love of man, thereby equating sacrifice, and mortification of the flesh, with love, which always struck me as a dangerous cocktail.

the lion of babylon

"Former Iraqi Detainees Allege Torture," *New York Times*, 14 November 2005.

Zoltan Istvan, "In Iraq, Urday Hussein's Lions Remain Victims of War," *National Geographic Today*, 2 October 2003.

note: The Colosseum began as a sacred site, perhaps with astronomical significance (like Stonehenge), yet ended with spectacles that included human sacrifice and dwarf-tossing—it could be argued that America, under Bush, moved into its dwarf-tossing phase.

note: The *New York Times*, shortly after the attacks of 11 September 2001, reported that the Pentagon had created a department of disinformation, in order to use the media as a tool in the soon-to-be-dubbed *War on Terror* (see Jessica Lynch, Pat Tillman, et al.).

a story that could be true
note: The photograph of Ali Shalal Qaissi appeared on the front page of the *New York Times* on 11 March 2006.

Errol Morris, "Will the *Real* Hooded Man Please Stand Up," *New York Times*(.com), 15 August 2007.

note: The Taguba Report documents the U.S. military investigation into the abuses at Abu Ghraib.

note: According to the logs from Abu Ghraib, Sabrina Harman spent a total of eleven days on tier 1A. Morris studied the timelines of the photographs, so it would be of interest to see if every photograph of a detainee on a box corresponds to one of the eleven days Harman was on tier 1A—even so, it would still be possible that Mr. Qaissi was put on a box another night and not photographed, or that the photograph was destroyed.

note: The dead Iraqi over whom Sabrina Harman was photographed giving a thumbs-up sign was named Manadel al-Jamadi. A photograph of al-Jamadi's ten-year-old son holding the photograph of Harman and his dead feather was published in *Newsweek* in 2006. Harman refers to al Jamadi simply as "The Iceman," since his body was packed in ice to prevent it from decomposing. The CIA interrogator considered responsible for al-Jamadi's death, Mark Swanner, now lives in the suburbs of Virginia.

the fruit of my deeds
note: Thich Nhat Hanh offers this meditation:

> Knowing that my deeds are my true belongings,
> I breathe in
> Knowing that I cannot escape the fruit of my deeds,
> I breathe out

Beth B, *Breathe In, Breathe Out* (film), 2000.

Walt Whitman, *Leaves of Grass*.

istanbul redux
Jane Mayer, *The Dark Side: The Inside Story of How the War on Terror Turned into a War on American Ideals* (Doubleday, 2008).

Mark Danner, *Torture and Truth: America, Abu Ghraib, and the War on Terror* (New York Review Books, 2004).

note: The Military Commissions Act of 2006 suspended habeus corpus (specifically for Guantánamo detainees—a provision struck down by the Supreme Court in 2008), allows evidence extracted by torture (euphemistically termed "coercion" in the bill) to be admitted as evidence (if obtained before May 2005), and allows the president to authorize the CIA, or anyone, to torture if deemed necessary for national security (or, to be precise, the bill authorized the president to "interpret the meaning and application of the Geneva Conventions," which in practice meant the president could, and did, unilaterally authorize interrogation techniques that many people consider torture).

standard operating procedure
Philip Gourevitch, *Standard Operating Procedure* (Penguin, 2008), pp. 136–49.

Physicians for Human Rights, *Broken Laws, Broken Lives*.

note: Graner, a former prison guard, was (perhaps) chosen to be on tier 1A precisely because he enjoyed brutalizing prisoners, so it's hard to believe that he was worried about an Iraqi's well-being, or that he was concerned that a cell wasn't clean enough for the next prisoner, but I could be wrong—we contain multitudes.

note: Anodyne (which translates to *capable of relieving pain*) is the (odd) word Gourevitch uses to describe the treatment of another man the MPs nicknamed "Shitboy"—both Morris and Gourevitch use these nicknames throughout both the film and the book, even though the Iraqis' real names are known, or they could have simply given them respectable aliases.

note: Former Army Sgt. Sam Provance was stationed at Abu Ghraib at the time the photographs were taken, and was interviewed by Morris for his film, yet his words ended up on the cutting room floor. Provance is "the only uniformed military intelligence officer at Abu Ghraib who broke the code of silence surrounding the infamous prisoner abuses. He spoke out during the Army's internal investigation, at a congressional hearing and in press interviews. Provance was punished and pushed out of the U.S. military, clearing the way for the Pentagon to pin the blame for the sadistic treatment of Iraqi detainees on a handful of poorly trained MPs." Provance feels that Morris's film "muddies the already opaque waters regarding who was actually responsible for the abuse of prisoners" (*Alternative News*, 1 May 2008).

wrong ocean
note: Lulu actually sleeps just fine—in our ignorance as new parents we didn't know infants need regular naps.

giddy-up
note: I took the silhouette down from my grandfather's wall once and saw someone else's name penciled on the back—even this shadow had nothing to do with me. Here's a transcription of one of my grandfather's deathbed visions:

> *There's no beginning, no end. Here is space, a great big thing, like this. What's on the other side of it? I probably believe somewhat in the holy spirit. Close that door—what's on the outside of it. And what's on the outside of that—it just goes on and on and on. I've been thinking of this for about 15 years. I come to a pretty good conclusion, then I come to*

an episode that destroys all conclusions. How can you put a limit on space? You can't. I've been dreaming about people once in a while—they haven't been chasing each other through the woods with knives—good people. Some facts are going to open up somewhere along the line because space can't go on forever. What's on the other side of it—it's impossible, it can't be. A dimension that will be exposed one day. There isn't any other side of it, it can't be, you turn your back and you look at a blank wall, but it can't be a blank wall. There's something on the other side of that. See those flowers?—I'm going to leave them there until tomorrow.

don't be cruel

Plato, *Republic*.

Dan Froomkin, "We Tortured and We'd Do It Again," *Washington Post*, 6 February 2008.

Philippe Sands, *The Torture Team* (Palgrave Macmillan, 2008).

note: The Hamdan case is fundamentally about whether the president can unilaterally set up a court system, without authorization from Congress, to prosecute "war on terror" detainees. The "military commissions" that Bush established (the rest of the world called them kangaroo courts) were set up, in part, to allow the use of evidence that was literally beaten out of the defendants and other detainees. The Supreme Court struck down these military commissions as unconstitutional, but a few months later

Congress reinstated them, only slightly altered, with the Military Commissions Act.

note: The Vatican, in May 2008, updated the Seven Deadly Sins—cruelty, for some reason, still doesn't make the list.

solaris (house of strange fathers)

Slavoj Zizek, *The Pervert's Guide to Cinema* (film).

Larry C. James, *Fixing Hell: An Army Psychologist Confronts Abu Ghraib* (Grand Central Publishing, 2008).

note: James is considered by many to be a torture apologist, in that he advocates for APA psychologists to be present during interrogations.

here comes the sun

note: As I write this a plane crash-lands in the Hudson River, and, miraculously, all 155 passengers and crew survive.

pond

note: Parenthetical lines in the first two sentences are from George Oppen's poem "Sara in Her Father's Arms."

the lord god bird

Dante, *Inferno* (my own translation).

note: Sightings of the ivory-billed woodpecker remain unsubstantiated.

[debts]

Grain upon grain   this book is a synthesis of many conversations, with both friends and strangers—poets and lawyers, carpenters and historians, military interrogators and former Iraqi detainees, human rights workers and investigative journalists—each offered daily sustenance, through word or gesture, when the way into these shadows was in no way clear. Some of the many who need to be named include: Bill Clegg, Jill Bialosky, Susan Burke, Daniel Heyman, and Ben Wizner—this book would not exist without your insights, indignation, brilliance, bewilderment, and goodwill. Also, earlier, inchoate versions of this book were wrestled into human form by: Tyler Cabot (*Esquire*); Joanna Yas and Thomas Beller (Open City), Ben George (*The Book of Dads*), Niko Hansen, Tim Jung, and Thomas Gunkel (Arche / Atrium), Lee Brackstone (Faber), and Adrienne Davich (along with all the shiny people at Norton)—impossible without you. Finally, behold Lili, who   *one day, suddenly*   offered a glimmer of a way out of these woods   *a heap, a little heap, the impossible heap*   before I was able.

[bragging rights]

Nick Flynn's *Another Bullshit Night in Suck City* (Norton, 2004) won the PEN/Martha Albrand Award, was shortlisted for France's Prix Femina, and has been translated into thirteen languages. He is also the author of a play, *Alice Invents a Little Game and Alice Always Wins* (Faber, 2008), as well as two books of poetry, *Some Ether* (Graywolf, 2000) and *Blind Huber* (Graywolf, 2002), for which he received fellowships from, among other organizations, the Guggenheim Foundation and the Library of Congress. Some of the venues in which his poems, essays, and nonfiction have appeared include the *New Yorker,* the *Paris Review,* National Public Radio's *This American Life,* and *The New York Times Book Review.* His film credits include "field poet" and artistic collaborator on the film *Darwin's Nightmare,* which was nominated for an Academy Award for best feature documentary in 2006. One semester a year he teaches at the University of Houston, and he then spends the rest of the year in Brooklyn.

(www.nickflynn.org)

[permissions]